Functional Programming in JavaScript

Unlock the powers of functional programming hidden within JavaScript to build smarter, cleaner, and more reliable web apps

Dan Mantyla

BIRMINGHAM - MUMBAI

Functional Programming in JavaScript

Copyright © 2015 Packt Publishing

All rights reserved. No part of this book may be reproduced, stored in a retrieval system, or transmitted in any form or by any means, without the prior written permission of the publisher, except in the case of brief quotations embedded in critical articles or reviews.

Every effort has been made in the preparation of this book to ensure the accuracy of the information presented. However, the information contained in this book is sold without warranty, either express or implied. Neither the author nor Packt Publishing, and its dealers and distributors will be held liable for any damages caused or alleged to be caused directly or indirectly by this book.

Packt Publishing has endeavored to provide trademark information about all of the companies and products mentioned in this book by the appropriate use of capitals. However, Packt Publishing cannot guarantee the accuracy of this information.

First published: March 2015

Production reference: 1230315

Published by Packt Publishing Ltd.
Livery Place
35 Livery Street
Birmingham B3 2PB, UK

ISBN 978-1-78439-822-4

`www.packtpub.com`

Cover Image by Dan Mantyla

Credits

Author
Dan Mantyla

Reviewers
Dom Derrien
Joe Dorocak
Peter Ehrlich
Edward E. Griebel Jr.

Commissioning Editor
Julian Ursell

Acquisition Editor
Owen Roberts

Content Development Editor
Kirti Patil

Technical Editor
Abhishek R. Kotian

Copy Editors
Aditya Nair
Aarti Saldanha
Vikrant Phadkey

Project Coordinator
Nidhi Joshi

Proofreaders
Stephen Copestake
Maria Gould
Paul Hindle

Indexer
Tejal Daruwale Soni

Production Coordinator
Aparna Bhagat

Cover Work
Aparna Bhagat

About the Author

Dan Mantyla works as a web application developer for the University of Kansas. He enjoys contributing to open source web frameworks and wrenching on motorcycles. Dan is currently living in Lawrence, Kansas, USA — the birthplace of Python Django and home to Linux News Media.

Dan has also clicked the cover image, which was taken outside his home in Lawrence, Kansas, USA, where the sunflower fields are in bloom for only one short week in September.

About the Reviewers

Dom Derrien is a full stack web developer who has recently been defining application environments with a focus on high availability and scalability. He's been in the development field for more than 15 years and has worked for big and small companies and as an entrepreneur.

He's currently working for the game company Ubisoft, where he defines the next generation services platform for its successful AAA games. To extend the gamer experience on to the Web and on mobiles, he provides technical means that are transparent, efficient, and highly flexible.

Having developed smart clients before the introduction of XHR, using a frameset tag to keep the context and a hidden frame of size=0 to dynamically exchange data with servers, he had a great pleasure of reviewing this book, which pushes the language to its limits. He hopes that it will help developers improve their programming skills.

> I want to thank my wife, Sophie, and our sons, Erwan and Goulven, with whom I enjoy a peaceful life in Montréal, Québec, Canada.

Joe Dorocak, whose Internet moniker is Joe Codeswell, is a very experienced programmer. He enjoys creating readable code that implements project requirements efficiently and in a manner that can be easily understood. He considers writing code akin to writing poetry.

Joe prides himself on the ability to communicate clearly and professionally. He considers his code to be communication, not only with the machine platforms on which it runs, but also with human programmers who might read it in the future.

Joe has worked as an employee as well as in a contractual role for major brands such as IBM, HP, GTE/Sprint, and other top-shelf companies. He is presently consulting on web, mobile, and desktop applications, which are coded primarily, but not exclusively, in Python and JavaScript. For more details about him, please visit `https://www.linkedin.com/in/joedorocak`.

Peter Ehrlich taught himself web programming in 2007, and now works on performance JavaScript and WebGL at Leap Motion, Inc. In his spare time, he enjoys dancing, rock climbing, and taking naps.

Edward E. Griebel Jr. has been developing enterprise software for over 20 years in C, C++, and Java. He has a bachelor of science degree in computer engineering. He is currently a middleware architect at a leading payroll and financial services provider in the U.S., focusing on systems integration and UI and server development.

www.PacktPub.com

Support files, eBooks, discount offers and more

For support files and downloads related to your book, please visit www.PacktPub.com.

Did you know that Packt offers eBook versions of every book published, with PDF and ePub files available? You can upgrade to the eBook version at www.PacktPub.com and as a print book customer, you are entitled to a discount on the eBook copy. Get in touch with us at service@packtpub.com for more details.

At www.PacktPub.com, you can also read a collection of free technical articles, sign up for a range of free newsletters and receive exclusive discounts and offers on Packt books and eBooks.

https://www2.packtpub.com/books/subscription/packtlib

Do you need instant solutions to your IT questions? PacktLib is Packt's online digital book library. Here, you can access, read and search across Packt's entire library of books.

Why Subscribe?
- Fully searchable across every book published by Packt
- Copy and paste, print and bookmark content
- On demand and accessible via web browser

Free Access for Packt account holders

If you have an account with Packt at www.PacktPub.com, you can use this to access PacktLib today and view nine entirely free books. Simply use your login credentials for immediate access.

Table of Contents

Preface	v
Chapter 1: The Powers of JavaScript's Functional Side – a Demonstration	1
Introduction	1
The demonstration	2
The application – an e-commerce website	2
Imperative methods	2
Functional programming	4
Summary	7
Chapter 2: Fundamentals of Functional Programming	9
Functional programming languages	9
What makes a language functional?	10
Advantages	11
Cleaner code	11
Modularity	12
Reusability	12
Reduced coupling	12
Mathematically correct	12
Functional programming in a nonfunctional world	14
Is JavaScript a functional programming language?	15
Working with functions	**17**
Self-invoking functions and closures	18
Higher-order functions	19
Pure functions	20
Anonymous functions	21
Method chains	23
Recursion	24
Divide and conquer	25
Lazy evaluation	26

The functional programmer's toolkit	**27**
Callbacks	28
Array.prototype.map()	29
Array.prototype.filter()	30
Array.prototype.reduce()	31
Honorable mentions	32
Array.prototype.forEach	32
Array.prototype.concat	33
Array.prototype.reverse	34
Array.prototype.sort	34
Array.prototype.every and Array.prototype.some	35
Summary	**35**
Chapter 3: Setting Up the Functional Programming Environment	**37**
Introduction	**37**
Functional libraries for JavaScript	**38**
Underscore.js	38
Fantasy Land	41
Bilby.js	42
Lazy.js	44
Bacon.js	45
Honorable mentions	46
Development and production environments	**48**
Browsers	48
Server-side JavaScript	49
A functional use case in the server-side environment	49
CLI	50
Using functional libraries with other JavaScript modules	50
Functional languages that compile into JavaScript	51
Summary	**52**
Chapter 4: Implementing Functional Programming Techniques in JavaScript	**53**
Partial function application and currying	**54**
Function manipulation	54
Apply, call, and the this keyword	54
Binding arguments	55
Function factories	56
Partial application	57
Partial application from the left	58
Partial application from the right	59
Currying	60

Function composition — 62
Compose — 62
Sequence – compose in reverse — 63
Compositions versus chains — 64
Programming with compose — 65
Mostly functional programming — 68
Handling events — 70
Functional reactive programming — 71
Reactivity — 72
Putting it all together — 73
Summary — 75

Chapter 5: Category Theory — 77
Category theory — 78
Category theory in a nutshell — 78
Type safety — 80
Object identities — 82
Functors — 83
Creating functors — 84
Arrays and functors — 84
Function compositions, revisited — 85
Monads — 87
Maybes — 88
Promises — 90
Lenses — 92
jQuery is a monad — 94
Implementing categories — 95
Summary — 98

Chapter 6: Advanced Topics and Pitfalls in JavaScript — 99
Recursion — 100
Tail recursion — 100
The Tail-call elimination — 101
Trampolining — 103
The Y-combinator — 106
Memoization — 108
Variable scope — 109
Scope resolutions — 109
Global scope — 110
Local scope — 110
Object properties — 111
Closures — 112
Gotchas — 113

Table of Contents

Function declarations versus function expressions versus the function constructor — **114**
- Function declarations — 114
- Function expressions — 115
- The function constructor — 115
- Unpredictable behavior — 116

Summary — **117**

Chapter 7: Functional and Object-oriented Programming in JavaScript — 119

- **JavaScript – the multi-paradigm language** — **120**
- **JavaScript's object-oriented implementation – using prototypes** — **121**
  - Inheritance — 121
  - JavaScript's prototype chain — 122
  - Inheritance in JavaScript and the Object.create() method — 123
- **Mixing functional and object-oriented programming in JavaScript** — **125**
  - Functional inheritance — 125
    - Strategy Pattern — 126
  - Mixins — 128
    - Classical mixins — 129
    - Functional mixins — 130
- **Summary** — **133**

Appendix A: Common Functions for Functional Programming in JavaScript — 135

Appendix B: Glossary of Terms — 143

Index — 147

Preface

Functional programming is a style that emphasizes and enables the writing of smarter code, which minimizes complexity and increases modularity. It's a way of writing cleaner code through clever ways of mutating, combining, and using functions. JavaScript provides an excellent medium for this approach. JavaScript, the Internet's scripting language, is actually a functional language at heart. By learning how to expose its true identity as a functional language, we can implement web applications that are powerful, easier to maintain, and more reliable. By doing this, JavaScript's odd quirks and pitfalls will suddenly become clear and the language as a whole will make infinitely more sense. Learning how to use functional programming will make you a better programmer for life.

This book is a guide for both new and experienced JavaScript developers who are interested in learning functional programming. With a focus on the progression of functional programming techniques, styles, and detailed information about JavaScript libraries, this book will help you to write smarter code and become a better programmer.

What this book covers

Chapter 1, *The Powers of JavaScript's Functional Side – a Demonstration*, sets the pace of the book by creating a small web application with the help of both traditional methods and functional programming. It then compares these two methods to underline the importance of functional programming.

Chapter 2, *Fundamentals of Functional Programming*, introduces you to the core concepts of functional programming as well as built-in JavaScript functions.

Chapter 3, *Setting Up the Functional Programming Environment*, explores different JavaScript libraries and how they can be optimized for functional programming.

Preface

Chapter 4, *Implementing Functional Programming Techniques in JavaScript*, explains the functional paradigm in JavaScript. It covers several styles of functional programming and demonstrates how they can be employed in different scenarios.

Chapter 5, *Category Theory*, explains the concept of Category Theory in detail and then implements it in JavaScript.

Chapter 6, *Advanced Topics and Pitfalls in JavaScript*, highlights various drawbacks you may face while programming in JavaScript, and the various ways to successfully deal with them.

Chapter 7, *Functional and Object-oriented Programming in JavaScript*, relates both functional and object-oriented programming to JavaScript, and shows you how the two paradigms can complement each other and coexist side by side.

Appendix A, *Common Functions for Functional Programming in JavaScript*, contains common functions used to perform functional programming in JavaScript.

Appendix B, *Glossary of Terms*, includes a glossary of terms used throughout the book.

What you need for this book

Only a browser is needed to get you up and running.

Who this book is for

If you are a JavaScript developer interested in learning functional programming, looking for a quantum leap toward mastering the JavaScript language, or just want to become a better programmer in general, then this book is ideal for you. This guide is aimed at programmers involved in developing reactive frontend applications, server-side applications that wrangle with reliability and concurrency, and everything else in between.

Conventions

In this book, you will find a number of text styles that distinguish between different kinds of information. Here are some examples of these styles and an explanation of their meaning.

Code words in text, database table names, folder names, filenames, file extensions, pathnames, dummy URLs, user input, and Twitter handles are shown as follows: "We can include other contexts through the use of the `include` directive."

A block of code is set as follows:

```
Function.prototype.partialApply = function() {
  var func = this;
  args = Array.prototype.slice.call(arguments);
  return function() {
    return func.apply(this, args.concat(
      Array.prototype.slice.call(arguments)
    ));
  };
};
```

When we wish to draw your attention to a particular part of a code block, the relevant lines or items are set in bold:

```
var messages = ['Hi', 'Hello', 'Sup', 'Hey', 'Hola'];
messages.map(function(s,i){
  return printSomewhere(s, i*10, i*10);
}).forEach(document.body.appendChild);
```

New terms and **important words** are shown in bold. Words that you see on the screen, for example, in menus or dialog boxes, appear in the text like this: "Clicking the **Next** button moves you to the next screen."

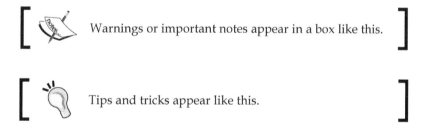

> Warnings or important notes appear in a box like this.

> Tips and tricks appear like this.

Reader feedback

Feedback from our readers is always welcome. Let us know what you think about this book—what you liked or disliked. Reader feedback is important for us as it helps us develop titles that you will really get the most out of.

To send us general feedback, simply e-mail `feedback@packtpub.com`, and mention the book's title in the subject of your message.

If there is a topic that you have expertise in and you are interested in either writing or contributing to a book, see our author guide at `www.packtpub.com/authors`.

Customer support

Now that you are the proud owner of a Packt book, we have a number of things to help you to get the most from your purchase.

Downloading the example code

You can download the example code files from your account at http://www.packtpub.com for all the Packt Publishing books you have purchased. If you purchased this book elsewhere, you can visit http://www.packtpub.com/support and register to have the files e-mailed directly to you.

Errata

Although we have taken every care to ensure the accuracy of our content, mistakes do happen. If you find a mistake in one of our books—maybe a mistake in the text or the code—we would be grateful if you could report this to us. By doing so, you can save other readers from frustration and help us improve subsequent versions of this book. If you find any errata, please report them by visiting http://www.packtpub.com/submit-errata, selecting your book, clicking on the **Errata Submission Form** link, and entering the details of your errata. Once your errata are verified, your submission will be accepted and the errata will be uploaded to our website or added to any list of existing errata under the Errata section of that title.

To view the previously submitted errata, go to https://www.packtpub.com/books/content/support and enter the name of the book in the search field. The required information will appear under the **Errata** section.

Piracy

Piracy of copyrighted material on the Internet is an ongoing problem across all media. At Packt, we take the protection of our copyright and licenses very seriously. If you come across any illegal copies of our works in any form on the Internet, please provide us with the location address or website name immediately so that we can pursue a remedy.

Please contact us at copyright@packtpub.com with a link to the suspected pirated material.

We appreciate your help in protecting our authors and our ability to bring you valuable content.

Questions

If you have a problem with any aspect of this book, you can contact us at `questions@packtpub.com`, and we will do our best to address the problem.

1
The Powers of JavaScript's Functional Side – a Demonstration

Introduction

For decades, functional programming has been the darling of computer science aficionados, prized for its mathematical purity and puzzling nature that kept it hidden in dusty computer labs occupied by data scientists and PhD hopefuls. But now, it is going through a resurgence, thanks to modern languages such as **Python**, **Julia**, **Ruby**, **Clojure** and—last but not least—**JavaScipt**.

JavaScript, you say? The web's scripting language? Yes!

JavaScript has proven to be an important technology that isn't going away for quite a while. This is largely due to the fact that it is capable of being reborn and extended with new frameworks and libraries, such as **backbone.js**, **jQuery**, **Dojo**, **underscore.js**, and many more. *This is directly related to JavaScript's true identity as a functional programming language.* An understanding of functional programming with JavaScript will be welcome and useful for a long time for programmers of any skill level.

Why so? Functional programming is very powerful, robust, and elegant. It is useful and efficient on large data structures. It can be very advantageous to use JavaScript—a client-side scripting language, as a functional means to manipulate the DOM, sort API responses or perform other tasks on increasingly complex websites.

In this book, you will learn everything you need to know about functional programming with JavaScript: how to empower your JavaScript web applications with functional programming, how to unlock JavaScript's hidden powers, and how to write better code that is both more powerful and — because it is smaller — easier to maintain, faster to download, and takes less overhead. You will also learn the core concepts of functional programming, how to apply them to JavaScript, how to side-step the caveats and issues that may arise when using JavaScript as a functional language, and how to mix functional programming with object-oriented programming in JavaScript.

But before we begin, let's perform an experiment.

The demonstration

Perhaps a quick demonstration will be the best way to introduce functional programming with JavaScript. We will perform the same task using JavaScript — once using traditional, native methods, and once with functional programming. Then, we will compare the two methods.

The application – an e-commerce website

In pursuit of a real-world application, let's say we need an e-commerce web application for a mail-order coffee bean company. They sell several types of coffee and in different quantities, both of which affect the price.

Imperative methods

First, let's go with the procedural route. To keep this demonstration down to earth, we'll have to create objects that hold the data. This allows the ability to fetch the values from a database if we need to. But for now, we'll assume they're statically defined:

```
// create some objects to store the data.
var columbian = {
  name: 'columbian',
  basePrice: 5
};
var frenchRoast = {
  name: 'french roast',
  basePrice: 8
};
var decaf = {
  name: 'decaf',
```

```
  basePrice: 6
};

// we'll use a helper function to calculate the cost
// according to the size and print it to an HTML list
function printPrice(coffee, size) {
  if (size == 'small') {
    var price = coffee.basePrice + 2;
  }
  else if (size == 'medium') {
    var price = coffee.basePrice + 4;
  }
  else {
    var price = coffee.basePrice + 6;
  }

// create the new html list item
  var node = document.createElement("li");
  var label = coffee.name + ' ' + size;
  var textnode = document.createTextNode(label+' price: $'+price);
  node.appendChild(textnode);
  document.getElementById('products').appendChild(node);
}

// now all we need to do is call the printPrice function
// for every single combination of coffee type and size
printPrice(columbian, 'small');
printPrice(columbian, 'medium');
printPrice(columbian, 'large');
printPrice(frenchRoast, 'small');
printPrice(frenchRoast, 'medium');
printPrice(frenchRoast, 'large');
printPrice(decaf, 'small');
printPrice(decaf, 'medium');
printPrice(decaf, 'large');
```

Downloading the example code

You can download example code files for all Packt books you have purchased from your account at http://www.packtpub.com. If you purchased this book elsewhere, you can visit http://www.packtpub.com/support and register to have the files e-mailed directly to you.

As you can see, this code is very basic. What if there were many more coffee styles than just the three we have here? What if there were 20? 50? What if, in addition to size, there were organic and non-organic options. That could increase the lines of code extremely quickly!

Using this method, we are telling the machine what to print for each coffee type and for each size. This is fundamentally what is wrong with imperative code.

Functional programming

While imperative code tells the machine, step-by-step, what it needs to do to solve the problem, functional programming instead seeks to describe the problem mathematically so that the machine can do the rest.

With a more functional approach, the same application can be written as follows:

```
// separate the data and logic from the interface
var printPrice = function(price, label) {
  var node = document.createElement("li");
  var textnode = document.createTextNode(label+' price: $'+price);
  node.appendChild(textnode);
  document.getElementById('products 2').appendChild(node);
}

// create function objects for each type of coffee
var columbian = function(){
  this.name = 'columbian';
  this.basePrice = 5;
};
var frenchRoast = function(){
  this.name = 'french roast';
  this.basePrice = 8;
};
var decaf = function(){
  this.name = 'decaf';
  this.basePrice = 6;
};

// create object literals for the different sizes
var small = {
  getPrice: function(){return this.basePrice + 2},
  getLabel: function(){return this.name + ' small'}
};
var medium = {
```

```
    getPrice: function(){return this.basePrice + 4},
    getLabel: function(){return this.name + ' medium'}
  };
  var large = {
    getPrice: function(){return this.basePrice + 6},
    getLabel: function(){return this.name + ' large'}
  };

  // put all the coffee types and sizes into arrays
  var coffeeTypes = [columbian, frenchRoast, decaf];
  var coffeeSizes = [small, medium, large];

  // build new objects that are combinations of the above
  // and put them into a new array
  var coffees = coffeeTypes.reduce(function(previous, current) {
    var newCoffee = coffeeSizes.map(function(mixin) {
      // `plusmix` function for functional mixins, see Ch.7
      var newCoffeeObj = plusMixin(current, mixin);
      return new newCoffeeObj();
    });
    return previous.concat(newCoffee);
  },[]);

  // we've now defined how to get the price and label for each
  // coffee type and size combination, now we can just print them
  coffees.forEach(function(coffee){
    printPrice(coffee.getPrice(),coffee.getLabel());
  });
```

The first thing that should be obvious is that it is much more modular. This makes adding a new size or a new coffee type as simple as shown in the following code snippet:

```
  var peruvian = function(){
    this.name = 'peruvian';
    this.basePrice = 11;
  };

  var extraLarge = {
    getPrice: function(){return this.basePrice + 10},
    getLabel: function(){return this.name + ' extra large'}
  };

  coffeeTypes.push(Peruvian);
  coffeeSizes.push(extraLarge);
```

Arrays of coffee objects and size objects are "mixed" together, — that is, their methods and member variables are combined — with a custom function called `plusMixin` (see *Chapter 7, Functional and Object-oriented Programming in JavaScript*). The coffee type classes contain the member variables and the sizes contain methods to calculate the name and price. The "mixing" happens within a map operation, which applies a pure function to each element in an array and returns a new function inside a `reduce()` operation — another higher-order function similar to the `map` function, except that all the elements in the array are combined into one. Finally, the new array of all possible combinations of types and sizes is iterated through with the `forEach()` method The `forEach()` method is yet another higher-order function that applies a callback function to each object in an array. In this example, we provide it as an anonymous function that instantiates the objects and calls the `printPrice()` function with the object's `getPrice()` and `getLabel()` methods as arguments.

Actually, we could make this example even more functional by removing the `coffees` variable and chaining the functions together — another little trick in functional programming.

```
coffeeTypes.reduce(function(previous, current) {
  var newCoffee = coffeeSizes.map(function(mixin) {
    // `plusMixin` function for functional mixins, see Ch.7
    var newCoffeeObj = plusMixin(current, mixin);
    return new newCoffeeObj();
  });
  return previous.concat(newCoffee);
}, []).forEach(function(coffee) {
  printPrice(coffee.getPrice(),coffee.getLabel());
});
```

Also, the control flow is not as top-to-bottom as the imperative code was. In functional programming, the `map()` function and other higher-order functions take the place of `for` and `while` loops and very little importance is placed on the order of execution. This makes it a little trickier for newcomers to the paradigm to read the code but, once you get the hang of it, it's not hard at all to follow and you'll see that it is much better.

This example barely touched on what functional programming can do in JavaScript. Throughout this book, you will see even more powerful examples of the functional approach.

Summary

First, the benefits of adopting a functional style are clear.

Second, don't be scared of functional programming. Yes, it is often thought of as pure logic in the form of computer language, but we don't need to understand **Lambda calculus** to be able to apply it to everyday tasks. The fact is, by allowing our programs to be broken down into smaller pieces, they're easier to understand, simpler to maintain, and more reliable. `map()` and `reduce()` function's are lesser-known built-in functions in JavaScript, but we'll look at them.

JavaScript is a scripting language, interactive and approachable. No compiling is necessary. We don't even need to download any development software, your favorite browser works as the interpreter and as the development environment.

Interested? Alright, let's get started!

2
Fundamentals of Functional Programming

By now, you've seen a small glimpse of what functional programming can do. But what exactly is functional programming? What makes one language functional and not another? What makes one programming style functional and not another?

In this chapter, we will first answer these questions and then cover the core concepts of functional programming:

- Using functions and arrays for control flow
- Writing pure functions, anonymous functions, recursive functions, and more
- Passing functions around like objects
- Utilizing the `map()`, `filter()`, and `reduce()` functions

Functional programming languages

Functional programming languages are languages that facilitate the functional programming paradigm. At the risk of oversimplifying, we could say that, if a language includes the features required for functional programming, then it is a functional language—as simple as that. In most cases, it's the programming style that truly determines whether a program is functional or not.

What makes a language functional?

Functional programming cannot be performed in C. Functional programming cannot be performed in Java (without a lot of cumbersome workarounds for "almost" functional programming). Those and many more languages simply don't contain the constructs to support it. They are purely object-oriented and strictly non-functional languages.

At the same time, object-oriented programming cannot be performed on purely functional languages, such as **Scheme**, **Haskell**, and **Lisp,** just to name a few.

However, there are certain languages that support both models. Python is a famous example, but there are others: Ruby, Julia, and—here's the one we're interested in—JavaScript. How can these languages support two design patterns that are very different from each other? They contain the features required for both programming paradigms. However, in the case of JavaScript, the functional features are somewhat hidden.

But really, it's a little more involved than that. So what makes a language functional?

Characteristic	**Imperative**	**Functional**
Programming Style	Perform step-by-step tasks and manage changes in state	Define what the problem is and what data transformations are needed to achieve the solution
State Changes	Important	Non-existent
Order of Execution	Important	Not as important
Primary Flow Control	Loops, conditionals, and function calls	Function calls and recursion
Primary Manipulation Unit	Structures and class objects	Functions as first-class objects and data sets

The syntax of the language must allow for certain design patterns, such as an inferred type system, and the ability to use anonymous functions. Essentially, the language must implement Lambda calculus. Also, the interpreter's evaluation strategy should be non-strict and call-by-need (also known as deferred execution), which allows for immutable data structures and non-strict, lazy evaluation.

Advantages

You could say that the profound enlightenment you experience when you finally "get it" will make learning functional programming worth it. An experience such as this will make you a better programmer for the rest of your life, whether you actually become a full-time functional programmer or not.

But we're not talking about learning to meditate; we're talking about learning an extremely useful tool that will make you a better programmer.

Formally speaking, what exactly are the practical advantages of using functional programming?

Cleaner code

Functional programs are cleaner, simpler, and smaller. This simplifies debugging, testing, and maintenance.

For example, let's say we need a function that converts a two-dimensional array into a one-dimensional array. Using only imperative techniques, we could write it the following way:

```
function merge2dArrayIntoOne(arrays) {
  var count = arrays.length;
  var merged = new Array(count);
  var c = 0;
  for (var i = 0; i < count; ++i) {
    for (var j = 0, jlen = arrays[i].length; j < jlen; ++j) {
      merged[c++] = arrays[i][j];
    }
  }
  return merged
}
```

And using functional techniques, it could be written as follows:

```
varmerge2dArrayIntoOne2 = function(arrays) {
  return arrays.reduce( function(p,n){
    return p.concat(n);
  });
};
```

Both of these functions take the same input and return the same output. However, the functional example is much more concise and clean.

Modularity

Functional programming forces large problems to be broken down into smaller instances of the same problem to be solved. This means that the code is more modular. Programs that are modular are clearly specified, easier to debug, and simpler to maintain. Testing is easier because each piece of modular code can potentially be checked for correctness.

Reusability

Functional programs share a variety of common helper functions, due to the modularity of functional programming. You'll find that many of these functions can be reused for a variety of different applications.

Many of the most common functions will be covered later in this chapter. However, as you work as a functional programmer, you will inevitably compile your own library of little functions that can be used over and over again. For example, a well-designed function that searches through the lines of a configuration file could also be used to search through a hash table.

Reduced coupling

Coupling is the amount of dependency between modules in a program. Because the functional programmer works to write first-class, higher-order, pure functions that are completely independent of each other with no side effects on global variables, coupling is greatly reduced. Certainly, functions will unavoidably rely on each other. But modifying one function will not change another, so long as the one-to-one mapping of inputs to outputs remains correct.

Mathematically correct

This last one is on a more theoretical level. Thanks to its roots in Lambda calculus, functional programs can be mathematically proven to be correct. This is a big advantage for researchers who need to prove the growth rate, time complexity, and mathematical correctness of a program.

Let's look at Fibonacci's sequence. Although it's rarely used for anything other than a proof-of-concept, it illustrates this concept quite well. The standard way of evaluating a Fibonacci sequence is to create a recursive function that expresses `fibonnaci(n) = fibonnaci(n-2) + fibonnaci(n-1)` with a base case to `return 1` when `n < 2`, which makes it possible to stop the recursion and begin adding up the values returned at each step in the recursive call stack.

This describes the intermediary steps involved in calculating the sequence.

```
var fibonacci = function(n) {
  if (n < 2) {
    return 1;
  }
  else {
    return fibonacci(n - 2) + fibonacci(n - 1);
  }
}
console.log( fibonacci(8) );
// Output: 34
```

However, with the help of a library that implements a lazy execution strategy, an indefinite sequence can be generated that states the *mathematical equation* that defines the entire sequence of numbers. Only as many numbers as needed will be computed.

```
var fibonacci2 = Lazy.generate(function() {
  var x = 1,
  y = 1;
  return function() {
    var prev = x;
    x = y;
    y += prev;
    return prev;
  };
}());

console.log(fibonacci2.length());// Output: undefined

console.log(fibonacci2.take(12).toArray());// Output: [1, 1, 2, 3, 5, 8, 13, 21, 34, 55, 89, 144]

var fibonacci3 = Lazy.generate(function() {
  var x = 1,
  y = 1;
  return function() {
    var prev = x;
    x = y;
    y += prev;
    return prev;
  };
}());

console.log(fibonacci3.take(9).reverse().first(1).toArray());//
Output: [34]
```

The second example is clearly more mathematically sound. It relies on the `Lazy.js` library of JavaScript. There are other libraries that can help here as well, such as `Sloth.js` and `wu.js`. These will be covered in *Chapter 3, Setting Up the Functional Programming Environment*.

Functional programming in a nonfunctional world

Can functional and nonfunctional programming be mixed together? Although this is the subject of *Chapter 7, Functional & Object-oriented Programming in JavaScript*, it is important to get a few things straight before we go any further.

This book is not intended to teach you how to implement an entire application that strictly adheres to the rigors of pure functional programming. Such applications are rarely appropriate outside Academia. Rather, this book will teach you how to use functional programming design strategies within your applications to complement the necessary imperative code.

For example, if you need the first four words that only contain letters out of some text, they could naively be written like this:

```
var words = [], count = 0;
text = myString.split(' ');
for (i=0; count<4, i<text.length; i++) {
  if (!text[i].match(/[0-9]/)) {
    words = words.concat(text[i]);
    count++;
  }
}
console.log(words);
```

In contrast, a functional programmer might write them as follows:

```
var words = [];
var words = myString.split(' ').filter(function(x){
  return (! x.match(/[1-9]+/));
}).slice(0,4);
console.log(words);
```

Or, with a library of functional programming utilities, they can be simplified even further:

```
var words = toSequence(myString).match(/[a-zA-Z]+/).first(4);
```

The key to identifying functions that can be written in a more functional way is to look for loops and temporary variables, such as `words` and `count` instances in the preceding example. We can usually do away with both temporary variables and loops by replacing them with higher-order functions, which we will explore later in this chapter.

Is JavaScript a functional programming language?

There is one last question we must ask ourselves. Is JavaScript a functional language or a non-functional language?

JavaScript is arguably the world's most popular and least understood functional programming language. JavaScript is a functional programming language in C-like clothing. Its syntax is undeniably C-like, meaning it uses C's block syntax and in-fix ordering. And it's one of the worst named languages in existence. It doesn't take a lot of imagination to see how so many people can confuse JavaScript as being related to Java; somehow, its name implies that it should be! But in reality it has very little in common with Java. And, to really cement the idea that JavaScript is an object-oriented language, libraries and frameworks such as Dojo and **ease.js** have been hard at work attempting to abstract it and make it suitable for object-oriented programming. JavaScript came of age in the 1990s when OOP was all the buzz, and we've been told that JavaScript is object-oriented because we want it to be so badly. But it is not.

Its true identity is much more aligned with its ancestors: Scheme and Lisp, two classic functional languages. JavaScript is a functional language, all the way. Its functions are first-class and can be nested, it has closures and compositions, and it allows for currying and monads. All of these are key to functional programming. Here are a few more reasons why JavaScript is a functional language:

- JavaScript's lexical grammar includes the ability to pass functions as arguments, has an inferred type system, and allows for anonymous functions, higher-order functions, closures and more. These facts are paramount to achieving the structure and behavior of functional programming.

- It is not a pure object-oriented language, with most object-oriented design patterns achieved by copying the Prototype object, a weak model for object-oriented programming. **European Computer Manufacturers Association Script (ECMAScript)**, JavaScript's formal and standardized specifications for implementation, states the following in specification 4.2.1:

  "ECMAScript does not contain proper classes such as those in C++, Smalltalk, or Java, but rather, supports constructors which create objects. In a class-based object-oriented language, in general, state is carried by instances, methods are carried by classes, and inheritance is only of structure and behavior. In ECMAScript, the state and methods are carried by objects, and structure, behavior and state are all inherited."

- It is an interpreted language. Sometimes called "engines", JavaScript interpreters often closely resemble Scheme interpreters. Both are dynamic, both have flexible datatypes that easily combine and transform, both evaluate the code into blocks of expressions, and both treat functions similarly.

That being said, it is true that JavaScript is not a pure functional language. What's lacking is lazy evaluation and built-in immutable data. This is because most interpreters are call-by-name and not call-by-need. JavaScript also isn't very good with recursion due to the way it handles tail calls. However, all of these issues can be mitigated with a little bit of attention. Non-strict evaluation, required for infinite sequences and lazy evaluation, can be achieved with a library called `Lazy.js`. Immutable data can be achieved simply by programming technique, but this requires more programmer discipline rather than relying on the language to take care of it. And recursive tail call elimination can be achieved with a method called **Trampolining**. These issues will be addressed in *Chapter 6, Advanced Topics & Pitfalls in JavaScript*.

Many debates have been waged over whether or not JavaScript is a functional language, an object-oriented language, both, or neither. And this won't be the last debate.

In the end, functional programming is way of writing cleaner code through clever ways of mutating, combining, and using functions. And JavaScript provides an excellent medium for this approach. If you really want to use JavaScript to its full potential, you must learn how to use it as a functional language.

Working with functions

> *Sometimes, the elegant implementation is a function. Not a method. Not a class. Not a framework. Just a function.*
>
> *-John Carmack, lead programmer of the Doom video game*

Functional programming is all about decomposing a problem into a set of functions. Often, functions are chained together, nested within each other, passed around, and treated as first-class citizens. If you've used frameworks such as jQuery and Node.js, you've probably used some of these techniques, you just didn't realize it!

Let's start with a little JavaScript dilemma.

Say we need to compile a list of values that are assigned to generic objects. The objects could be anything: dates, HTML objects, and so on.

```
var
  obj1 = {value: 1},
  obj2 = {value: 2},
  obj3 = {value: 3};

var values = [];
function accumulate(obj) {
  values.push(obj.value);
}
accumulate(obj1);
accumulate(obj2);
console.log(values); // Output: [obj1.value, obj2.value]
```

It works but it's volatile. Any code can modify the `values` object without calling the `accumulate()` function. And if we forget to assign the empty set, `[]`, to the `values` instance then the code will not work at all.

But if the variable is declared inside the function, it can't be mutated by any rogue lines of code.

```
function accumulate2(obj) {
  var values = [];
  values.push(obj.value);
  return values;
}
console.log(accumulate2(obj1)); // Returns: [obj1.value]
console.log(accumulate2(obj2)); // Returns: [obj2.value]
console.log(accumulate2(obj3)); // Returns: [obj3.value]
```

It does not work! Only the value of the object last passed in is returned.

We could possibly solve this with a nested function inside the first function.

```
var ValueAccumulator = function(obj) {
  var values = []
  var accumulate = function() {
    values.push(obj.value);
  };
  accumulate();
  return values;
};
```

But it's the same issue, and now we cannot reach the `accumulate` function or the `values` variable.

What we need is a self-invoking function.

Self-invoking functions and closures

What if we could return a function expression that in-turn returns the `values` array? Variables declared in a function are available to any code within the function, including self-invoking functions.

By using a self-invoking function, our dilemma is solved.

```
var ValueAccumulator = function() {
  var values = [];
  var accumulate = function(obj) {
    if (obj) {
      values.push(obj.value);
      return values;
    }
    else {
      return values;
    }
  };
  return accumulate;
};

//This allows us to do this:
var accumulator = ValueAccumulator();
accumulator(obj1);
accumulator(obj2);
console.log(accumulator());
// Output: [obj1.value, obj2.value]
```

It's all about variable scoping. The `values` variable is available to the inner `accumulate()` function, even when code outside the scope calls the functions. This is called a closure.

 Closures in JavaScript are functions that have access to the parent scope, even when the parent function has closed.

Closures are a feature of all functional languages. Traditional imperative languages do not allow them.

Higher-order functions

Self-invoking functions are actually a form of higher-order functions. Higher-order functions are functions that either take another function as the input or return a function as the output.

Higher-order functions are not common in traditional programming. While an imperative programmer might use a loop to iterate an array, a functional programmer would take another approach entirely. By using a higher-order function, the array can be worked on by applying that function to each item in the array to create a new array.

This is the central idea of the functional programming paradigm. What higher-order functions allow is the ability to pass logic to other functions, just like objects.

Functions are treated as first-class citizens in JavaScript, a distinction JavaScript shares with Scheme, Haskell, and the other classic functional languages. This may sound bizarre, but all this really means is that functions are treated as primitives, just like numbers and objects. If numbers and objects can be passed around, so can functions.

To see this in action, let's use a higher-order function with our `ValueAccumulator()` function from the previous section:

```
// using forEach() to iterate through an array and call a
// callback function, accumulator, for each item
var accumulator2 = ValueAccumulator();
var objects = [obj1, obj2, obj3]; // could be huge array of objects
objects.forEach(accumulator2);
console.log(accumulator2());
```

Pure functions

Pure functions return a value computed using only the inputs passed to it. Outside variables and global states may not be used and there may be no side effects. In other words, it must not mutate the variables passed to it for input. Therefore, pure functions are only used for their returned value.

A simple example of this is a math function. The `Math.sqrt(4)` function will always return 2, does not use any hidden information such as settings or state, and will never inflict any side effects.

Pure functions are the true interpretation of the mathematical term for 'function', a relation between inputs and an output. They are simple to think about and are readily re-usable. Because they are totally independent, pure functions are more capable of being used again and again.

To illustrate this, compare the following non-pure function to the pure one.

```javascript
// function that prints a message to the center of the screen
var printCenter = function(str) {
  var elem = document.createElement("div");
  elem.textContent = str;
  elem.style.position = 'absolute';
  elem.style.top = window.innerHeight/2+"px";
  elem.style.left = window.innerWidth/2+"px";
  document.body.appendChild(elem);
};
printCenter('hello world');
// pure function that accomplishes the same thing
var printSomewhere = function(str, height, width) {
  var elem = document.createElement("div");
  elem.textContent = str;
  elem.style.position = 'absolute';
  elem.style.top = height;
  elem.style.left = width;
  return elem;
};
document.body.appendChild(
  printSomewhere('hello world',
  window.innerHeight/2)+10+"px",
  window.innerWidth/2)+10+"px")
);
```

While the non-pure function relies on the state of the window object to compute the height and width, the pure, self-sufficient function instead asks that those values be passed in. What this actually does is allow the message to be printed anywhere, and this makes the function much more versatile.

And while the non-pure function may seem like the easier option because it performs the appending itself instead of returning an element, the pure function `printSomewhere()` and its returned value play better with other functional programming design techniques.

```
var messages = ['Hi', 'Hello', 'Sup', 'Hey', 'Hola'];
messages.map(function(s,i){
  return printSomewhere(s, 100*i*10, 100*i*10);
}).forEach(function(element) {
  document.body.appendChild(element);
});
```

When the functions are pure and don't rely on state or environment, then we don't care about when or where they actually get computed. We'll see this later with lazy evaluation.

Anonymous functions

Another benefit of treating functions as first-class objects is the advent of anonymous functions.

As the name might imply, anonymous functions are functions without names. But they are more than that. What they allow is the ability to define ad-hoc logic, on-the-spot and as needed. Usually, it's for the benefit of convenience; if the function is only referred to once, then a variable name doesn't need to be wasted on it.

Some examples of anonymous functions are as follows:

```
// The standard way to write anonymous functions
function(){return "hello world"};

// Anonymous function assigned to variable
var anon = function(x,y){return x+y};

// Anonymous function used in place of a named callback function,
// this is one of the more common uses of anonymous functions.
setInterval(function(){console.log(new Date().getTime())}, 1000);
```

```
// Output:  1413249010672, 1413249010673, 1413249010674, ...

// Without wrapping it in an anonymous function, it immediately
// execute once and then return undefined as the callback:
setInterval(console.log(new Date().getTime()), 1000)
// Output:  1413249010671
```

A more involved example of anonymous functions used within higher-order functions:

```
function powersOf(x) {
  return function(y) {
    // this is an anonymous function!
    return Math.pow(x,y);
  };
}
powerOfTwo = powersOf(2);
console.log(powerOfTwo(1)); // 2
console.log(powerOfTwo(2)); // 4
console.log(powerOfTwo(3)); // 8

powerOfThree = powersOf(3);
console.log(powerOfThree(3));  // 9
console.log(powerOfThree(10)); // 59049
```

The function that is returned doesn't need to be named; it can't be used anywhere outside the powersOf() function, and so it is an anonymous function.

Remember our accumulator function? It can be re-written using anonymous functions.

```
var
  obj1 = {value: 1},
  obj2 = {value: 2},
  obj3 = {value: 3};

var values = (function() {
  // anonymous function
  var values = [];
  return function(obj) {
    // another anonymous function!
    if (obj) {
      values.push(obj.value);
      return values;
    }
    else {
```

```
            return values;
        }
    }
})(); // make it self-executing
console.log(values(obj1)); // Returns: [obj.value]
console.log(values(obj2)); // Returns: [obj.value, obj2.value]
```

Right on! A pure, high-order, anonymous function. How did we ever get so lucky? Actually, it's more than that. It's also *self-executing* as indicated by the structure, `(function(){...})();`. The pair of parentheses following the anonymous function causes the function to be called right away. In the above example, the `values` instance is assigned to the output of the self-executing function call.

> Anonymous functions are more than just syntactical sugar. They are the embodiment of Lambda calculus. Stay with me on this... Lambda calculus was invented long before computers or computer languages. It was just a mathematical notion for reasoning about functions. Remarkably, it was discovered that—despite the fact that it only defines three kinds of expressions: variable references, function calls, and *anonymous functions*—it was Turing-complete. Today, Lambda calculus lies at the core of all functional languages if you know how to find it, including JavaScript.
>
> For this reason, anonymous functions are often called lambda expressions.

One drawback to anonymous functions remains. They're difficult to identify in call stacks, which makes debugging trickier. They should be used sparingly.

Method chains

Chaining methods together in JavaScript is quit common. If you've used jQuery, you've likely performed this technique. It's sometimes called the "Builder Pattern".

It's a technique that is used to simplify code where multiple functions are applied to an object one after another.

```
// Instead of applying the functions one per line...
arr = [1,2,3,4];
arr1 = arr.reverse();
arr2 = arr1.concat([5,6]);
arr3 = arr2.map(Math.sqrt);
```

Fundamentals of Functional Programming

```
// ...they can be chained together into a one-liner
console.log([1,2,3,4].reverse().concat([5,6]).map(Math.sqrt));
// parentheses may be used to illustrate
console.log(((([1,2,3,4]).reverse()).concat([5,6])).map(Math.sqrt)
);
```

This only works when the functions are methods of the object being worked on. If you created your own function that, for example, takes two arrays and returns an array with the two arrays zipped together, you must declare it as a member of the `Array.prototype` object. Take a look at the following code snippet:

```
Array.prototype.zip = function(arr2) {
  // ...
}
```

This would allow us to the following:

```
arr.zip([11,12,13,14]).map(function(n){return n*2});
// Output: 2, 22, 4, 24, 6, 26, 8, 28
```

Recursion

Recursion is likely the most famous functional programming technique. If you don't know by now, a recursive function is a function that calls itself.

When a functions calls *itself*, something strange happens. It acts both as a loop, in that it executes the same code multiple times, and as a function stack.

Recursive functions must be very careful to avoid an infinite loop (rather, infinite recursion in this case). So just like loops, a condition must be used to know when to stop. This is called the base case.

An example is as follows:

```
var foo = function(n) {
  if (n < 0) {
    // base case
    return 'hello';
  }
  else {
    // recursive case
    foo(n-1);
  }
}
console.log(foo(5));
```

It's possible to convert any loop to a recursive algorithm and any recursive algorithm to a loop. But recursive algorithms are more appropriate, almost necessary, for situations that differ greatly from those where loops are appropriate.

A good example is tree traversal. While it's not too hard to traverse a tree using a recursive function, a loop would be much more complex and would need to maintain a stack. And that would go against the spirit of functional programming.

```
var getLeafs = function(node) {
  if (node.childNodes.length == 0) {
    // base case
    return node.innerText;
  }
  else {
    // recursive case:
    return node.childNodes.map(getLeafs);
  }
}
```

Divide and conquer

Recursion is more than an interesting way to iterate without `for` and `while` loops. An algorithm design, known as divide and conquer, recursively breaks problems down into smaller instances of the same problem until they're small enough to solve.

The historical example of this is the Euclidan algorithm for finding the greatest common denominator for two numbers.

```
function gcd(a, b) {
  if (b == 0) {
    // base case (conquer)
    return a;
  }
  else {
    // recursive case (divide)
    return gcd(b, a % b);
  }
}

console.log(gcd(12,8));
console.log(gcd(100,20));
```

So in theory, divide and conquer works quite eloquently, but does it have any use in the real world? Yes! The JavaScript function for sorting arrays is not very good. Not only does it sort the array in place, which means that the data is not immutable, but it is unreliable and inflexible. With divide and conquer, we can do better.

The merge sort algorithm uses the divide and conquer recursive algorithm design to efficiently sort an array by recursively dividing the array into smaller sub-arrays and then merging them together.

The full implementation in JavaScript is about 40 lines of code. However, pseudo-code is as follows:

```
var mergeSort = function(arr){
  if (arr.length < 2) {
    // base case: 0 or 1 item arrays don't need sorting
    return items;
  }
  else {
    // recursive case: divide the array, sort, then merge
    var middle = Math.floor(arr.length / 2);
    // divide
    var left = mergeSort(arr.slice(0, middle));
    var right = mergeSort(arr.slice(middle));
    // conquer
    // merge is a helper function that returns a new array
    // of the two arrays merged together
    return merge(left, right);
  }
}
```

Lazy evaluation

Lazy evaluation, also known as non-strict evaluation, call-by-need and deffered execution, is an evaluation strategy that waits until the value is needed to compute the result of a function and is particularly useful for functional programming. It's clear that a line of code that states x = func() is calling for x to be assigned to the returned value by func(). But what x actually equates to does not matter until it is needed. Waiting to call func() until x is needed is known as lazy evaluation.

This strategy can result in a major increase in performance, especially when used with method chains and arrays, the favorite program flow techniques of the functional programmer.

One exciting benefit of lazy evaluation is the existence of infinite series. Because nothing is actually computed until it can't be delayed any further, it's possible to do this:

```
// wishful JavaScript pseudocode:
var infinateNums = range(1 to infinity);
var tenPrimes = infinateNums.getPrimeNumbers().first(10);
```

This opens the door for many possibilities: asynchronous execution, parallelization, and composition, just to name a few.

However, there's one problem: JavaScript does not perform Lazy evaluation on its own. That being said, there exist libraries for JavaScript that simulate lazy evaluation very well. That is the subject of *Chapter 3, Setting Up the Functional Programming Environment*.

The functional programmer's toolkit

If you've looked closely at the few examples presented so far, you'll notice a few methods being used that you may not be familiar with. They are the `map()`, `filter()`, and `reduce()` functions, and they are crucial to every functional program of any language. They enable you to remove loops and statements, resulting in cleaner code.

The `map()`, `filter()`, and `reduce()` functions make up the core of the functional programmer's toolkit, a collection of pure, higher-order functions that are the workhorses of the functional method. In fact, they're the epitome of what a pure function and what a higher-order function should be like; they take a function as input and return an output with zero side effects.

While they're standard for browsers that implement ECMAScript 5.1, they only work on arrays. Each time it's called, a new array is created and returned. The existing array is not modified. But there's more, *they take functions as inputs*, often in the form of anonymous functions referred to as callback functions; they iterate over the array and apply the function to each item in the array!

```
myArray = [1,2,3,4];
newArray = myArray.map(function(x) {return x*2});
console.log(myArray);  // Output: [1,2,3,4]
console.log(newArray); // Output: [2,4,6,8]
```

One more thing. Because they only work on arrays, they do not work on other iterable data structures, like certain objects. Fret not, libraries such as `underscore.js`, `Lazy.js`, `stream.js`, and many more all implement their own `map()`, `filter()`, and `reduce()` methods that are more versatile.

Callbacks

If you've never worked with callbacks before, you might find the concept a little puzzling. This is especially true in JavaScript, given the several different ways that JavaScript allows you to declare functions.

A `callback()` function is used for passing to other functions for them to use. It's a way to pass logic just as you would pass an object:

```
var myArray = [1,2,3];
function myCallback(x){return x+1};
console.log(myArray.map(myCallback));
```

To make it simpler for easy tasks, anonymous functions can be used:

```
console.log(myArray.map(function(x){return x+1}));
```

They are not only used in functional programming, they are used for many things in JavaScript. Purely for example, here's a `callback()` function used in an AJAX call made with jQuery:

```
function myCallback(xhr){
   console.log(xhr.status);
   return true;
}
$.ajax(myURI).done(myCallback);
```

Notice that only the name of the function was used. And because we're not calling the callback and are only passing the name of it, it would be wrong to write this:

```
$.ajax(myURI).fail(myCallback(xhr));
// or
$.ajax(myURI).fail(myCallback());
```

What would happen if we did call the callback? In that case, the `myCallback(xhr)` method would try to execute—'undefined' would be printed to the console and it would return `True`. When the `ajax()` call completes, it will have 'true' as the name of the callback function to use, and that will throw an error.

What this also means is that we cannot specify what arguments are passed to the callback functions. If we need different parameters from what the `ajax()` call will pass to it, we can wrap the callback function in an anonymous function:

```
function myCallback(status){
  console.log(status);
  return true;
}
$.ajax(myURI).done(function(xhr){myCallback(xhr.status)});
```

Array.prototype.map()

The `map()` function is the ringleader of the bunch. It simply applies the callback function on each item in the array.

Syntax: `arr.map(callback [, thisArg]);`

Parameters:

- `callback()`: This function produces an element for the new array, receiving these arguments:
    - `currentValue`: This argument gives the current element being processed in the array
    - `index`: This argument gives the index of the current element in the array
    - `array`: This argument gives the array being processed
- `thisArg()`: This function is optional. The value is used as `this` when executing `callback`.

Examples:

```
var
  integers = [1,-0,9,-8,3],
  numbers = [1,2,3,4],
  str = 'hello world how ya doing?';
// map integers to their absolute values
console.log(integers.map(Math.abs));

// multiply an array of numbers by their position in the array
```

Fundamentals of Functional Programming

```
    console.log(numbers.map(function(x, i){return x*i}) );

    // Capitalize every other word in a string.
    console.log(str.split(' ').map(function(s, i){
      if (i%2 == 0) {
        return s.toUpperCase();
      }
      else {
        return s;
      }
    }) );
```

> While the Array.prototype.map method is a standard method for the Array object in JavaScript, it can be easily extended to your custom objects as well.
>
> ```
>     MyObject.prototype.map = function(f) {
>       return new MyObject(f(this.value));
>     };
> ```

Array.prototype.filter()

The `filter()` function is used to take elements out of an array. The callback must return `True` (to include the item in the new array) or `False` (to drop it). Something similar could be achieved by using the `map()` function and returning a `null` value for items you want dropped, but the `filter()` function will delete the item from the new array instead of inserting a `null` value in its place.

> Syntax: `arr.filter(callback [, thisArg]);`

Parameters:

- `callback()`: This function is used to test each element in the array. Return `True` to keep the element, `False` otherwise. With these parameters:
    - `currentValue`: This parameter gives the current element being processed in the array
    - `index`: This parameter gives the index of the current element in the array

- `array`: This parameter gives the array being processed.
- `thisArg()`: This function is optional. Value is used as `this` when executing `callback`.

Examples:

```
var myarray = [1,2,3,4]
words = 'hello 123 world how 345 ya doing'.split(' ');
re = '[a-zA-Z]';
// remove all negative numbers
console.log([-2,-1,0,1,2].filter(function(x){return x>0}));
// remove null values after a map operation
console.log(words.filter(function(s){
  return s.match(re);
}) );
// remove random objects from an array
console.log(myarray.filter(function(){
  return Math.floor(Math.random()*2) })
);
```

Array.prototype.reduce()

Sometimes called fold, the `reduce()` function is used to accumulate all the values of the array into one. The callback needs to return the logic to be performed to combine the objects. In the case of numbers, they're usually added together to get a sum or multiplied together to get a product. In the case of strings, the strings are often appended together.

 Syntax: `arr.reduce(callback [, initialValue]);`

Parameters:

- `callback()`: This function combines two objects into one, which is returned. With these parameters:
    - `previousValue`: This parameter gives the value previously returned from the last invocation of the callback, or the `initialValue`, if supplied
    - `currentValue`: This parameter gives the current element being processed in the array

- ◦ `index`: This parameter gives the index of the current element in the array
- ◦ `array`: This parameter gives the array being processed
- `initialValue()`: This function is optional. Object to use as the first argument to the first call of the `callback`.

Examples:

```
var numbers = [1,2,3,4];
// sum up all the values of an array
console.log([1,2,3,4,5].reduce(function(x,y){return x+y}, 0));
// sum up all the values of an array
console.log([1,2,3,4,5].reduce(function(x,y){return x+y}, 0));

// find the largest number
console.log(numbers.reduce(function(a,b){
  return Math.max(a,b)}) // max takes two arguments
);
```

Honorable mentions

The `map()`, `filter()`, and `reduce()` functions are not alone in our toolbox of helper functions. There exist many more functions that can be plugged into nearly any functional application.

Array.prototype.forEach

Essentially the non-pure version of `map()`, `forEach()` iterates over an array and applies a `callback()` function over each item. However, it doesn't return anything. It's a cleaner way of performing a `for` loop.

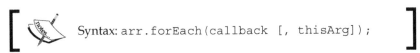

Syntax: `arr.forEach(callback [, thisArg]);`

Parameters:

- `callback()`: This function is to be performed for each value of the array. With these parameters:
    - `currentValue`: This parameter gives the current element being processed in the array
    - `index`: This parameter gives the index of the current element in the array
    - `array`: This parameter gives the array being processed
- `thisArg`: This function is optional. Value is used as `this` when executing `callback`.

Examples:

```
var arr = [1,2,3];
var nodes = arr.map(function(x) {
  var elem = document.createElement("div");
  elem.textContent = x;
  return elem;
});

// log the value of each item
arr.forEach(function(x){console.log(x)});

// append nodes to the DOM
nodes.forEach(function(x){document.body.appendChild(x)});
```

Array.prototype.concat

When working with arrays instead of `for` and `while` loops, often you will need to join multiple arrays together. Another built-in JavaScript function, `concat()`, takes care of this for us. The `concat()` function returns a new array and leaves the old arrays untouched. It can join as many arrays as you pass to it.

```
console.log([1, 2, 3].concat(['a','b','c']) // concatenate two arrays);
// Output: [1, 2, 3, 'a','b','c']
```

Fundamentals of Functional Programming

The original array is untouched. It returns a new array with both arrays concatenated together. This also means that the `concat()` function can be chained together.

```
var arr1 = [1,2,3];
var arr2 = [4,5,6];
var arr3 = [7,8,9];
var x = arr1.concat(arr2, arr3);
var y = arr1.concat(arr2).concat(arr3));
var z = arr1.concat(arr2.concat(arr3)));
console.log(x);
console.log(y);
console.log(z);
```

Variables x, y and z all contain [1,2,3,4,5,6,7,8,9].

Array.prototype.reverse

Another native JavaScript function helps with array transformations. The `reverse()` function inverts an array, such that the first element is now the last and the last is now the first.

However, it does not return a new array; instead it mutates the array in place. We can do better. Here's an implementation of a pure method for reversing an array:

```
var invert = function(arr) {
  return arr.map(function(x, i, a) {
    return a[a.length - (i+1)];
  });
};
var q = invert([1,2,3,4]);
console.log( q );
```

Array.prototype.sort

Much like our `map()`, `filter()`, and `reduce()` methods, the `sort()` method takes a `callback()` function that defines how the objects within an array should be sorted. But, like the `reverse()` function, it mutates the array in place. And that's no bueno.

```
arr = [200, 12, 56, 7, 344];
console.log(arr.sort(function(a,b){return a-b}) );
// arr is now: [7, 12, 56, 200, 344];
```

We could write a pure `sort()` function that doesn't mutate the array, but sorting algorithms is the source of much grief. Significantly large arrays that need to be sorted really should be organized in data structures that are designed just for that: quickStort, mergeSort, bubbleSort, and so on.

Array.prototype.every and Array.prototype.some

The `Array.prototype.every()` and `Array.prototype.some()` functions are both pure and high-order functions that are methods of the `Array` object and are used to test the elements of an array against a `callback()` function that must return a Boolean representing the respective input. The `every()` function returns `True` if the `callback()` function returns `True` for every element in the array, and the `some()` function returns `True` if some elements in the array are `True`.

Example:

```
function isNumber(n) {
  return !isNaN(parseFloat(n)) && isFinite(n);
}

console.log([1, 2, 3, 4].every(isNumber)); // Return: true
console.log([1, 2, 'a'].every(isNumber)); // Return: false
console.log([1, 2, 'a'].some(isNumber)); // Return: true
```

Summary

In order to develop an understanding of functional programming, this chapter covered a fairly broad range of topics. First we analyzed what it means for a programming language to be functional, then we evaluated JavaScript for its functional programming capabilities. Next, we applied the core concepts of functional programming using JavaScript and showcased some of JavaScript's built-in functions for functional programming.

Although JavaScript does have a few tools for functional programming, its functional core remains mostly hidden and much is to be desired. In the next chapter, we will explore several libraries for JavaScript that expose its functional underbelly.

3
Setting Up the Functional Programming Environment

Introduction

Do we need to know advanced math—category theory, Lambda calculus, polymorphisms—just to write applications with functional programming? Do we need to reinvent the wheel? The short answer to both these questions is *no*.

In this chapter, we will do our best to survey everything that can impact the way we write our functional applications in JavaScript.

- Libraries
- Toolkits
- Development environments
- Functional language that compiles to JavaScript
- And more

Please understand that the current landscape of functional libraries for JavaScript is a very fluid one. Like all aspects of computer programming, the community can change in a heartbeat; new libraries can be adopted and old ones can be abandoned. For instance, during the writing process of this very book, the popular and stable Node.js platform for I/O has been forked by its open source community. Its future is vague.

Therefore, the most important concept to be gained from this chapter is not how to use the current libraries for functional programming, but how to use any library that enhances JavaScript's functional programming method. This chapter will not focus on just one or two libraries, but will explore as many as possible with the goal of surveying all the many styles of functional programming that exist within JavaScript.

Functional libraries for JavaScript

It's been said that every functional programmer writes their own library of functions, and functional JavaScript programmers are no exception. With today's open source code-sharing platforms such as GitHub, Bower, and NPM, it's easier to share, collaborate, and grow these libraries. Many libraries exist for functional programming with JavaScript, ranging from tiny toolkits to monolithic module libraries.

Each library promotes its own style of functional programming. From a rigid, math-based style to a relaxed, informal style, each library is different but they all share one common feature: they all have abstract JavaScript functional capabilities to increase code re-use, readability, and robustness.

At the time of writing, however, a single library has not established itself as the de-facto standard. Some might argue that underscore.js is the one but, as you'll see in the following section, it might be advisable to avoid underscore.js.

Underscore.js

Underscore has become the standard functional JavaScript library in the eyes of many. It is mature, stable, and was created by *Jeremy Ashkenas*, the man behind the Backbone.js and CoffeeScript libraries. Underscore is actually a reimplementation of Ruby's Enumerable module, which explains why CoffeeScript was also influenced by Ruby.

Similar to jQuery, Underscore doesn't modify native JavaScript objects and instead uses a symbol to define its own object: the underscore character "_". So, using Underscore would work like this:

```
var x = _.map([1,2,3], Math.sqrt); // Underscore's map function
console.log(x.toString());
```

We've already seen JavaScrip's native map() method for the Array object, which works like this:

```
var x = [1,2,3].map(Math.sqrt);
```

The difference is that, in Underscore, both the `Array` object and the `callback()` function are passed as parameters to the Underscore object's `map()` method (`_.map`), as opposed to passing only the callback to the array's native `map()` method (`Array.prototype.map`).

But there's way more than just `map()` and other built-in functions to Underscore. It's full of super handy functions such as `find()`, `invoke()`, `pluck()`, `sortyBy()`, `groupBy()`, and more.

```
var greetings = [{origin: 'spanish', value: 'hola'},
{origin: 'english', value: 'hello'}];
console.log(_.pluck(greetings, 'value')  );
// Grabs an object's property.
// Returns: ['hola', 'hello']
console.log(_.find(greetings, function(s) {return s.origin == 'spanish';}));
// Looks for the first obj that passes the truth test
// Returns: {origin: 'spanish', value: 'hola'}
greetings = greetings.concat(_.object(['origin','value'], ['french','bonjour']));
console.log(greetings);
// _.object creates an object literal from two merged arrays
// Returns: [{origin: 'spanish', value: 'hola'},
//{origin: 'english', value: 'hello'},
//{origin: 'french', value: 'bonjour'}]
```

And it provides a way of chaining methods together:

```
var g = _.chain(greetings)
  .sortBy(function(x) {return x.value.length})
  .pluck('origin')
  .map(function(x){return x.charAt(0).toUpperCase()+x.slice(1) })
  .reduce(function(x, y){return x + ' ' + y}, '')
  .value();
// Applies the functions
// Returns: 'Spanish English French'
console.log(g);
```

> The `_.chain()` method returns a wrapped object that holds all the Underscore functions. The `_.value` method is then used to extract the value of the wrapped object. Wrapped objects are also very useful for mixing Underscore with object-oriented programming.

Despite its ease of use and adaptation by the community, the underscore.js library has been criticized for forcing you to write overly verbose code and for encouraging the wrong patterns. Underscore's structure may not be ideal or even function!

Until version 1.7.0, released shortly after Brian Lonsdorf's talk entitled *Hey Underscore, you're doing it wrong!*, landed on YouTube, Underscore explicitly prevented us from extending functions such as map(), reduce(), filter(), and more.

```
_.prototype.map = function(obj, iterate, [context]) {
  if (Array.prototype.map && obj.map === Array.prototype.map)
  return obj.map(iterate, context);
  // ...
};
```

 You can watch the video of Brian Lonsdorf's talk at www.youtube.com/watch?v=m3svKOdZij.

Map, in terms of category theory, is a homomorphic functor interface (more on this in *Chapter 5, Category Theory*). And we should be able to define map as a functor for whatever we need it for. So that's not very functional of Underscore.

And because JavaScript doesn't have built-in immutable data, a functional library should be careful to not allow its helper functions to mutate the objects passed to it. A good example of this problem is shown below. The intention of the snippet is to return a new selected list with one option set as the default. But what actually happens is that the selected list is mutated in place.

```
function getSelectedOptions(id, value) {
  options = document.querySelectorAll('#' + id + ' option');
  var newOptions = _.map(options, function(opt){
    if (opt.text == value) {
      opt.selected = true;
      opt.text += ' (this is the default)';
    }
    else {
      opt.selected = false;
    }
    return opt;
  });
  return newOptions;
}
var optionsHelp = getSelectedOptions('timezones', 'Chicago');
```

We would have to insert the line `opt = opt.cloneNode();` to the `callback()` function to make a copy of each object within the list being passed to the function. Underscore's `map()` function cheats to boost performance, but it is at the cost of functional *feng shui*. The native `Array.prototype.map()` function wouldn't require this because it makes a copy, but it also doesn't work on `nodelist` collections.

Underscore may be less than ideal for mathematically-correct, functional programming, but it was never intended to extend or transform JavaScript into a pure functional language. It defines itself as *a JavaScript library that provides a whole mess of useful functional programming helpers*. It may be a little more than a spurious collection of functional-like helpers, but it's no serious functional library either.

Is there a better library out there? Perhaps one that is based on mathematics?

Fantasy Land

Sometimes, the truth is stranger than fiction.

Fantasy Land is a collection of functional base libraries and a formal specification for how to implement "algebraic structures" in JavaScript. More specifically, Fantasy Land specifies the interoperability of common algebraic structures, or algebras for short: monads, monoids, setoids, functors, chains, and more. Their names may sound scary, but they're just a set of values, a set of operators, and some laws it must obey. In other words, they're just objects.

Here's how it works. Each algebra is a separate Fantasy Land specification and may have dependencies on other algebras that need to be implemented.

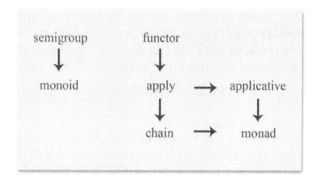

Some of the algebra specifications are:

- Setoids:
    - Implement the reflexivity, symmetry and transitivity laws
    - Define the `equals()` method

- Semigroups
    - Implement the associativity law
    - Define the `concat()` method

- Monoid
    - Implement right identity and left identity
    - Define the `empty()` method

- Functor
    - Implement the identity and composition laws
    - Define the `map()` method

The list goes on and on.

We don't necessarily need to know exactly what each algebra is for but it certainly helps, especially if you're writing your own library that conforms to the specifications. It's not just abstract nonsense, it outlines a means of implementing a high-level abstraction called category theory. A full explanation of category theory can be found in *Chapter 5, Category Theory*.

Fantasy Land doesn't just tell us how to implement functional programming, it does provide a set of functional modules for JavaScript. However, many are incomplete and documentation is pretty sparse. But Fantasy Land isn't the only library out there to implement its open source specifications. Others have too, namely: **Bilby.js**.

Bilby.js

What the heck is a bilby? No, it's not a mythical creature that might exist in Fantasy Land. It exists here on Earth as a freaky/cute cross between a mouse and a rabbit. Nonetheless, `bibly.js` library is compliant with Fantasy Land specifications.

In fact, `bilby.js` is a serious functional library. As its documentation states, it is, *Serious, meaning it applies category theory to enable highly abstract code. Functional, meaning it enables referentially transparent programs*. Wow, that is pretty serious. The documentation located at http://bilby.brianmckenna.org/ goes on to say that it provides:

- Immutable multi-methods for ad-hoc polymorphism
- Functional data structures
- Operator overloading for functional syntax
- Automated specification testing (**ScalaCheck**, **QuickCheck**)

By far the most mature library that conforms to the Fantasy Land specifications for algebraic structures, `Bilby.js` is a great resource for fully committing to the functional style.

Let's try an example:

```javascript
// environments in bilby are immutable structure for multimethods
var shapes1 = bilby.environment()
  // can define methods
  .method(
    'area', // methods take a name
    function(a){return typeof(a) == 'rect'}, // a predicate
    function(a){return a.x * a.y} // and an implementation
  )
  // and properties, like methods with predicates that always
  // return true
  .property(
     'name',   // takes a name
     'shape'); // and a function
// now we can overload it
var shapes2 = shapes1
  .method(
    'area', function(a){return typeof(a) == 'circle'},
    function(a){return a.r * a.r * Math.PI} );
var shapes3 = shapes2
  .method(
    'area', function(a){return typeof(a) == 'triangle'},
    function(a){return a.height * a.base / 2} );

// and now we can do something like this
var objs = [{type:'circle', r:5}, {type:'rect', x:2, y:3}];
var areas = objs.map(shapes3.area);

// and this
var totalArea = objs.map(shapes3.area).reduce(add);
```

This is category theory and ad-hoc polymorphism in action. Again, category theory will be covered in full in *Chapter 5, Category Theory*.

 Category theory is a recently invigorated branch of mathematics that functional programmers use to maximize the abstraction and usefulness of their code. *But there is a major drawback: it's difficult to conceptualize and quickly get started with.*

The truth is that Bilby and Fantasy Land are really stretching the possibilities of functional programming in JavaScript. Although it's exciting to see the evolution of computer science, the world may just not be ready for the kind of hard-core functional style that Bibly and Fantasy Land are pushing.

Maybe such a grandiose library on the bleeding-edge of functional JavaScript is not our thing. After all, we set out to explore the functional techniques that complement JavaScript, not to build functional programming dogma. Let's turn our attention to another new library, `Lazy.js`.

Lazy.js

Lazy is a utility library more along the lines of the `underscore.js` library but with a lazy evaluation strategy. Because of this, Lazy makes the impossible possible by functionally computing results of series that won't be available with immediate interpretation. It also boasts a significant performance boost.

The `Lazy.js` library is still very young. But it has a lot of momentum and community enthusiasm behind it.

The idea is that, in Lazy, everything is a sequence that we can iterate over. Owing to the way the library controls the order in which methods are applied, many really cool things can be achieved: asynchronous iteration (parallel programming), infinite sequences, functional reactive programming, and more.

The following examples show off a bit of everything:

```
// Get the first eight lines of a song's lyrics
var lyrics = "Lorem ipsum dolor sit amet, consectetur adipiscing eli
// Without Lazy, the entire string is first split into lines
console.log(lyrics.split('\n').slice(0,3));

// With Lazy, the text is only split into the first 8 lines
// The lyrics can even be infinitely long!
console.log(Lazy(lyrics).split('\n').take(3));
```

```
//First 10 squares that are evenly divisible by 3
var oneTo1000 = Lazy.range(1, 1000).toArray();
var sequence = Lazy(oneTo1000)
  .map(function(x) { return x * x; })
  .filter(function(x) { return x % 3 === 0; })
  .take(10)
  .each(function(x) { console.log(x); });

// asynchronous iteration over an infinite sequence
var asyncSequence = Lazy.generate(function(x){return x++})
  .async(100) // 0.100s intervals between elements
  .take(20) // only compute the first 20
  .each(function(e) { // begin iterating over the sequence
    console.log(new Date().getMilliseconds() + ": " + e);
});
```

More examples and use-cases are covered in *Chapter 4, Implementing Functional Programming Techniques in JavaScript*.

But its not entirely correct to fully credit the Lazy.js library with this idea. One of its predecessors, the Bacon.js library, works in much the same way.

Bacon.js

The logo of Bacon.js library is as follows:

The mustachioed hipster of functional programming libraries, Bacon.js is itself a library for *functional reactive programming*. Functional reactive programming just means that functional design patterns are used to represent values that are reactive and always changing, like the position of the mouse on the screen, or the price of a company's stock. In the same way that Lazy can get away with creating infinite sequences by not calculating the value until it's needed, Bacon can avoid having to calculate ever-changing values until the very last second.

Setting Up the Functional Programming Environment

What are called sequences in Lazy are known as EventStreams and Properties in Bacon because they're more suited for working with events (`onmouseover`, `onkeydown`, and so on) and reactive properties (scroll position, mouse position, toggles, and so on).

```
Bacon.fromEventTarget(document.body, "click")
  .onValue(function() { alert("Bacon!") });
```

Bacon is a little bit older than Lazy but its feature set is about half the size and its community enthusiasm is about equal.

Honorable mentions

There are simply too many libraries out there to do them all justice within the scope of this book. Let's look at a few more libraries for functional programming in JavaScript.

- `Functional`
    - Possibly the first library for functional programming in JavaScript, `Functional` is a library that includes comprehensive higher-order function support as well as `string` lambdas

- `wu.js`
    - Especially prized for its `curryable()` function, `wu.js` library is a very nice Library for functional programming. It was the first library (that I know of) to implement lazy evaluation, getting the ball rolling for `Bacon.js`, `Lazy.js` and other libraries
    - Yes, it is named after the infamous rap group *Wu Tang Clan*

- `sloth.js`
    - Very similar to the `Lazy.js` libraries, but much smaller

- `stream.js`
    - The `stream.js` library supports infinite streams and not much else
    - Absolutely tiny in size

- `Lo-Dash.js`
    - As the name might imply, the `lo-dash.js` library was inspired by the `underscore.js` library
    - Highly optimized

- `Sugar`
    - `Sugar` is a support library for functional programming techniques in JavaScript, like Underscore, but with some key differences in how it's implemented.
    - Instead of doing `_.pluck(myObjs, 'value')` in Underscore, it's just `myObjs.map('value')` in Sugar. This means that it modifies native JavaScript objects, so there is a small risk of it not playing nicely with other libraries that do the same such as Prototype.
    - Very good documentation, unit tests, analyzers, and more.
- `from.js`
    - A new functional library and **LINQ (Language Integrated Query)** engine for JavaScript that supports most of the same LINQ functions that .NET provides
    - 100% lazy evaluation and supports lambda expressions
    - Very young but documentation is excellent
- JSLINQ
    - Another functional LINQ engine for JavaScript
    - Much older and more mature than `from.js` library
- `Boiler.js`
    - Another utility library that extends JavaScript's functional methods to more primitives: strings, numbers, objects, collections and arrays
- **Folktale**
    - Like the `Bilby.js` library, Folktale is another new library that implements the Fantasy Land specifications. And like its forefather, Folktale is also a collection of libraries for functional programming in JavaScript. It's very young but could have a bright future.
- **jQuery**
    - Surprised to see jQuery mentioned here? Although jQuery is not a tool used to perform functional programming, it nevertheless is functional itself. jQuery might be one of the most widely used libraries that has its roots in functional programming.
    - The jQuery object is actually a monad. jQuery uses the monadic laws to enable method chaining:

        ```
        $('#mydiv').fadeIn().css('left': 50).alert('hi!');
        ```

A full explanation of this can be found in *Chapter 7, Functional and Object-oriented Programming in JavaScript*.

- And some of its methods are higher-order:

  ```
  $('li').css('left': function(index){return index*50});
  ```

- As of jQuery 1.8, the `deferred.then` parameter implements a functional concept known as Promises.

- jQuery is an abstraction layer, mainly for the DOM. It's not a framework or a toolkit, just a way to use abstraction to increase code-reuse and reduce ugly code. And isn't that what functional programming is all about?

Development and production environments

It does not matter in terms of programming style what type of environment the application is being developed in and will be deployed in. But it does matter to the libraries a lot.

Browsers

The majority of JavaScript applications are designed to run on the client side, that is, in the client's browser. Browser-based environments are excellent for development because browsers are ubiquitous, you can work on the code right on your local machine, the interpreter is the browser's JavaScript engine, and all browsers have a developer console. Firefox's FireBug provides very useful error messages and allows for break-points and more, but it's often helpful to run the same code in Chrome and Safari to cross-reference the error output. Even Internet Explorer contains developer tools.

The problem with browsers is that they evaluate JavaScript differently! Though it's not common, it is possible to write code that returns very different results in different browsers. But usually the differences are in the way they treat the document object model and not how prototypes and functions work. Obviously, `Math.sqrt(4)` method returns 2 to all browsers and shells. But the `scrollLeft` method depends on the browser's layout policies.

Writing browser-specific code is a waste of time, and that's another reason why libraries should be used.

Server-side JavaScript

The `Node.js` library has become the standard platform for creating server-side and network-based applications. Can functional programming be used for server-side application programming? Yes! Ok, but do there exist any functional libraries that are designed for this performance-critical environment? The answer to that is also: yes.

All the functional libraries outlined in this chapter will work in the `Node.js` library, and many depend on the `browserify.js` module to work with browser elements.

A functional use case in the server-side environment

In our brave new world of network systems, server-side application developers are often concerned with concurrency, and rightly so. The classic example is an application that allows multiple users to modify the same file. But if they try to modify it at the same time, you will get into an ugly mess. This is the *maintenance of state* problem that has plagued programmers for decades.

Assume the following scenario:

1. One morning, Adam opens a report for editing but he doesn't save it before leaving for lunch.
2. Billy opens the same report, adds his notes, and then saves it.
3. Adam comes back from lunch, adds his notes to the report, and then saves it, unknowingly overwriting Billy's notes.
4. The next day, Billy finds out that his notes are missing. His boss yells at him; everybody gets mad and they gang up on the misguided application developer who unfairly loses his job.

For a long time, the solution to this problem was to create a state about the file. Toggle a lock status to *on* when someone begins editing it, which prevents others from being able to edit it, and then toggle it to *off* once they save it. In our scenario, Billy would not be able to do his work until Adam gets back from lunch. And if it's never saved (if, say, Adam decided to quit his job in the middle of the lunch break), then no one will ever be able to edit it.

This is where functional programming's ideas about immutable data and state (or lack thereof) can really be put to work. Instead of having users modify the file directly, with a functional approach they would modify a copy of the file, which is a new revision. If they go to save the revision and a new revision already exists, then we know that someone else has already modified the old one. Crisis averted.

Now the scenario from before would unfold like this:

1. One morning, Adam opens a report for editing. But he doesn't save it before going to lunch.
2. Billy opens the same report, adds his notes, and saves it as a new revision.
3. Adam returns from lunch to add his notes. When he attempts to save the new revision, the application tells him that a newer revision now exists.
4. Adam opens the new revisions, adds his notes to it, and saves another new revision.
5. By looking at the revision history, the boss sees that everything is working smoothly. Everyone is happy and the application developer gets a promotion and a raise.

This is known as *event sourcing*. There is no explicit state to be maintained, only events. The process is much cleaner and there is a clear history of events that can be reviewed.

This idea and many others are why functional programming in server-side environments is on the rise.

CLI

Although web and the `node.js` library are the two main JavaScript environments, some pragmatic and adventurous users are finding ways to use JavaScript in the command line.

Using JavaScript as a **Command Line Interface** (**CLI**) scripting language might be one of the best opportunities to apply function programming. Imagine being able to use lazy evaluation when searching for local files or to rewrite an entire bash script into a functional JavaScript one-liner.

Using functional libraries with other JavaScript modules

Web applications are made up of all sorts of things: frameworks, libraries, APIs and more. They can work along side each other as dependents, plugins, or just as coexisting objects.

- `Backbone.js`
    - An **MVP (model-view-provider)** framework with a RESTful JSON interface
    - Requires the `underscore.js` library, Backbone's only hard dependency
- jQuery
    - The `Bacon.js` library has bindings for mixing with jQuery
    - Underscore and jQuery complement each other very well
- Prototype JavaScript Framework
    - Provides JavaScript with collection functions in the manner closest to Ruby's Enumerable
- `Sugar.js`
    - Modifies native objects and their methods
    - Must be careful when mixing with other libraries, especially Prototype

Functional languages that compile into JavaScript

Sometimes the thick veneer of C-like syntax over JavaScript's inner functionality can be enough to make you want to switch to another functional language. Well, you can!

- Clojure and ClojureScript
    - Closure is a modern Lisp implementation and a full-featured functional language
    - ClojureScript trans-compiles Clojure into JavaScript
- CoffeeScript
    - CoffeeScript is the name of both a functional language and a compiler for trans-compiling the language into JavaScript
    - 1-to-1 mapping between expressions in CoffeeScript and expression in JavaScript

There are many more out there, including **Pyjs**, **Roy**, **TypeScript**, **UHC** and more.

Summary

Which library you choose to use depends on what your needs are. Need functional reactive programming to handle events and dynamic values? Use the `Bacon.js` library. Only need infinite streams and nothing else? Use the `stream.js` library. Want to complement jQuery with functional helpers? Try the `underscore.js` library. Need a structured environment for serious ad hoc polymorphism? Check out the `bilby.js` library. Need a well-rounded tool for functional programming? Use the `Lazy.js` library. Not happy with any of these options? Write your own!

Any library is only as good as the way it's used. Although a few of the libraries outlined in this chapter have a few flaws, most faults occur somewhere between the keyboard and the chair. It's up to you to use the libraries correctly and to suit your needs.

And if we're importing code libraries into our JavaScript environment, then maybe we can import ideas and principles too. Maybe we can channel *The Zen of Python*, by *Tim Peter*:

Beautiful is better than ugly
Explicit is better than implicit.
Simple is better than complex.
Complex is better than complicated.
Flat is better than nested.
Sparse is better than dense.
Readability counts.
Special cases aren't special enough to break the rules.
Although practicality beats purity.
Errors should never pass silently.
Unless explicitly silenced.
In the face of ambiguity, refuse the temptation to guess.
There should be one – and preferably only one – obvious way to do it.
Although that way may not be obvious at first unless you're Dutch.
Now is better than never.
Although never is often better than "right" now.
If the implementation is hard to explain, it's a bad idea.
If the implementation is easy to explain, it may be a good idea.
Namespaces are one honking great idea – let's do more of those!

4
Implementing Functional Programming Techniques in JavaScript

Hold on to your hats because we're really going to get into the functional mind-set now.

In this chapter, we're going to do the following:

- Put all the core concepts together into a cohesive paradigm
- Explore the beauty that functional programming has to offer when we fully commit to the style
- Step through the logical progression of functional patterns as they build upon each other
- All the while, we will build up a simple application that does some pretty cool stuff

You may have noticed a few concepts that were brought up in the last chapter when dealing with functional libraries for JavaScript, but not in *Chapter 2, Fundamentals of Functional Programming*. Well, that was for a reason! Compositions, currying, partial application, and more. Let's explore why and how these libraries implemented those concepts.

Functional programming can come in a variety of flavors and patterns. This chapter will cover many different styles of functional programming:

- Data generic programming
- Mostly functional programming
- Functional reactive programming and more

This chapter, however, will be as style-unbiased as possible. Without leaning too hard on one style of functional programming over another, the overall goal is to show that there are better ways to write code than what is often accepted as the correct and only way. Once you free your mind about the preconceptions of what is the right way and what is not the right way to write code, you can do whatever you want. When you just write code with childlike abandon for no reason other than the fact that you like it and when you're not concerned about conforming to the traditional way of doing things, then the possibilities are endless.

Partial function application and currying

Many languages support optional arguments, but not in JavaScript. JavaScript uses a different pattern entirely that allows for any number of arguments to be passed to a function. This leaves the door open for some very interesting and unusual design patterns. Functions can be applied in part or in whole.

Partial application in JavaScript is the process of binding values to one or more arguments of a function that returns another function that accepts the remaining, unbound arguments. Similarly, currying is the process of transforming a function with many arguments into a function with one argument that returns another function that takes more arguments as needed.

The difference between the two may not be clear now, but it will be obvious in the end.

Function manipulation

Actually, before we go any further and explain just how to implement partial application and currying, we need a review. If we're going to tear JavaScript's thick veneer of C-like syntax right off and expose it's functional underbelly, then we're going to need to understand how primitives, functions, and prototypes in JavaScript work; we would never need to consider these if we just wanted to set some cookies or validate some form fields.

Apply, call, and the this keyword

In pure functional languages, functions are not invoked; they're applied. JavaScript works the same way and even provides utilities for manually calling and applying functions. And it's all about the `this` keyword, which, of course, is the object that the function is a member of.

The call() function lets you define the this keyword as the first argument. It works as follows:

```
console.log(['Hello', 'world'].join(' ')) // normal way
console.log(Array.prototype.join.call(['Hello', 'world'], ' ')); // using call
```

The call() function can be used, for example, to invoke anonymous functions:

```
console.log((function(){console.log(this.length)}).call([1,2,3]));
```

The apply() function is very similar to the call() function, but a little more useful:

```
console.log(Math.max(1,2,3)); // returns 3
console.log(Math.max([1,2,3])); // won't work for arrays though
console.log(Math.max.apply(null, [1,2,3])); // but this will work
```

The fundamental difference is that, while the call() function accepts a list of arguments, the apply() function accepts an array of arguments.

The call() and apply() functions allow you to write a function once and then inherit it in other objects without writing the function over again. And they are both members themselves of the Function argument.

> This is bonus material, but when you use the call() function on itself, some really cool things can happen:
> ```
> // these two lines are equivalent
> func.call(thisValue);
> Function.prototype.call.call(func, thisValue);
> ```

Binding arguments

The bind() function allows you to apply a method to one object with the this keyword assigned to another. Internally, it's the same as the call() function, but it's chained to the method and returns a new bounded function.

It's especially useful for callbacks, as shown in the following code snippet:

```
function Drum(){
  this.noise = 'boom';
  this.duration = 1000;
  this.goBoom = function(){console.log(this.noise)};
}
var drum = new Drum();
setInterval(drum.goBoom.bind(drum), drum.duration);
```

This solves a lot of problems in object-oriented frameworks, such as Dojo, specifically the problems of maintaining the state when using classes that define their own handler functions. But we can use the `bind()` function for functional programming too.

 The `bind()` function actually does partial application on its own, though in a very limited way.

Function factories

Remember our section on closures in *Chapter 2, Fundamentals of Functional Programming*? Closures are the constructs that makes it possible to create a useful JavaScript programming pattern known as function factories. They allow us to *manually bind* arguments to functions.

First, we'll need a function that binds an argument to another function:

```
function bindFirstArg(func, a) {
  return function(b) {
    return func(a, b);
  };
}
```

Then we can use this to create more generic functions:

```
var powersOfTwo = bindFirstArg(Math.pow, 2);
console.log(powersOfTwo(3)); // 8
console.log(powersOfTwo(5)); // 32
```

And it can work on the other argument too:

```
function bindSecondArg(func, b) {
  return function(a) {
    return func(a, b);
  };
}
var squareOf = bindSecondArg(Math.pow, 2);
var cubeOf = bindSecondArg(Math.pow, 3);
console.log(squareOf(3)); // 9
console.log(squareOf(4)); // 16
console.log(cubeOf(3));   // 27
console.log(cubeOf(4));   // 64
```

The ability to create generic functions is very important in functional programming. But there's a clever trick to making this process even more generalized. The bindFirstArg() function itself takes two arguments, the first being a function. If we pass the bindFirstArg function as a function to itself, we can create *bindable* functions. This can be best described with the following example:

```
var makePowersOf = bindFirstArg(bindFirstArg, Math.pow);
var powersOfThree = makePowersOf(3);
console.log(powersOfThree(2)); // 9
console.log(powersOfThree(3)); // 27
```

This is why they're called function factories.

Partial application

Notice that our function factory example's bindFirstArg() and bindSecondArg() functions only work for functions that have exactly two arguments. We could write new ones that work for different numbers of arguments, but that would work away from our model of generalization.

What we need is partial application.

Partial application is the process of binding values to one or more arguments of a function that returns a partially-applied function that accepts the remaining, unbound arguments.

Unlike the bind() function and other built-in methods of the Function object, we'll have to create our own functions for partial application and currying. There are two distinct ways to do this.

- As a stand-alone function, that is, var partial = function(func){...
- As a *polyfill*, that is, Function.prototype.partial = function(){...

Polyfills are used to augment prototypes with new functions and will allow us to call our new functions as methods of the function that we want to partially apply. Just like this: myfunction.partial(arg1, arg2, ...);

[57]

Partial application from the left

Here's where JavaScript's `apply()` and `call()` utilities become useful for us. Let's look at a possible polyfill for the Function object:

```
Function.prototype.partialApply = function(){
  var func = this;
  args = Array.prototype.slice.call(arguments);
  return function(){
    return func.apply(this, args.concat(
      Array.prototype.slice.call(arguments)
    ));
  };
};
```

As you can see, it works by slicing the `arguments` special variable.

> Every function has a special local variable called `arguments` that is an array-like object of the arguments passed to it. It's technically not an array. Therefore it does not have any of the Array methods such as `slice` and `forEach`. That's why we need to use Array's `slice.call` method to slice the arguments.

And now let's see what happens when we use it in an example. This time, let's get away from the math and go for something a little more useful. We'll create a little application that converts numbers to hexadecimal values.

```
function nums2hex() {
  function componentToHex(component) {
    var hex = component.toString(16);
    // make sure the return value is 2 digits, i.e. 0c or 12
    if (hex.length == 1) {
      return "0" + hex;
    }
    else {
      return hex;
    }
  }
  return Array.prototype.map.call(arguments,
  componentToHex).join('');
}

// the function works on any number of inputs
console.log(nums2hex()); // ''
console.log(nums2hex(100,200)); // '64c8'
```

```
console.log(nums2hex(100, 200, 255, 0, 123)); // '64c8ff007b'

// but we can use the partial function to partially apply
// arguments, such as the OUI of a mac address
var myOUI = 123;
var getMacAddress = nums2hex.partialApply(myOUI);
console.log(getMacAddress());  // '7b'
console.log(getMacAddress(100, 200, 2, 123, 66, 0, 1));
// '7b64c8027b420001'

// or we can convert rgb values of red only to hexadecimal
var shadesOfRed = nums2hex.partialApply(255);
console.log(shadesOfRed(123, 0));    // 'ff7b00'
console.log(shadesOfRed(100, 200));  // 'ff64c8'
```

This example shows that we can partially apply arguments to a generic function and get a new function in return. *This first example is left-to-right*, which means that we can only partially apply the first, left-most arguments.

Partial application from the right

In order to apply arguments from the right, we can define another polyfill.

```
Function.prototype.partialApplyRight = function(){
  var func = this;
  args = Array.prototype.slice.call(arguments);
  return function(){
    return func.apply(
      this,
      [].slice.call(arguments, 0)
      .concat(args));
  };
};

var shadesOfBlue = nums2hex.partialApplyRight(255);
console.log(shadesOfBlue(123, 0));    // '7b00ff'
console.log(shadesOfBlue(100, 200));  // '64c8ff'

var someShadesOfGreen = nums2hex.partialApplyRight(255, 0);
console.log(shadesOfGreen(123));   // '7bff00'
console.log(shadesOfGreen(100));   // '64ff00'
```

Partial application has allowed us to take a very generic function and extract more specific functions out of it. But the biggest flaw in this method is that the way in which the arguments are passed, as in how many and in what order, can be ambiguous. And ambiguity is never a good thing in programming. There's a better way to do this: currying.

Currying

Currying is the process of transforming a function with many arguments into a function with one argument that returns another function that takes more arguments as needed. Formally, a function with N arguments can be transformed into a function *chain* of N functions, each with only one argument.

A common question is: what is the difference between partial application and currying? While it's true that partial application returns a value right away and currying only returns another curried function that takes the next argument, the fundamental difference is that currying allows for much better control of how arguments are passed to the function. We'll see just how that's true, but first we need to create function to perform the currying.

Here's our polyfill for adding currying to the Function prototype:

```
Function.prototype.curry = function (numArgs) {
  var func = this;
  numArgs = numArgs || func.length;

  // recursively acquire the arguments
  function subCurry(prev) {
    return function (arg) {
      var args = prev.concat(arg);
      if (args.length < numArgs) {
        // recursive case: we still need more args
        return subCurry(args);
      }
      else {
        // base case: apply the function
        return func.apply(this, args);
      }
    };
  }
  return subCurry([]);
};
```

The `numArgs` argument lets us optionally specify the number of arguments the function being curried needs if it's not explicitly defined.

Let's look at how to use it within our hexadecimal application. We'll write a function that converts RGB values to a hexadecimal string that is appropriate for HTML:

```
function rgb2hex(r, g, b) {
  // nums2hex is previously defined in this chapter
  return '#' + nums2hex(r) + nums2hex(g) + nums2hex(b);
}
var hexColors = rgb2hex.curry();
console.log(hexColors(11)) // returns a curried function
console.log(hexColors(11,12,123)) // returns a curried function
console.log(hexColors(11)(12)(123)) // returns #0b0c7b
console.log(hexColors(210)(12)(0))   // returns #d20c00
```

It will return the curried function until all needed arguments are passed in. And they're passed in the same left-to-right order as defined by the function being curried.

But we can step it up a notch and define the more specific functions that we need as follows:

```
var reds   = function(g,b){return hexColors(255)(g)(b)};
var greens = function(r,b){return hexColors(r)(255)(b)};
var blues  = function(r,g){return hexColors(r)(g)(255)};
console.log(reds(11, 12))    // returns #ff0b0c
console.log(greens(11, 12))  // returns #0bff0c
console.log(blues(11, 12))   // returns #0b0cff
```

So that's a nice way to use currying. But if we just want to curry our `nums2hex()` function directly, we run into a little bit of trouble. And that's because the function doesn't define any arguments, it just lets you pass as many arguments in as you want. So we have to define the number of arguments. We do that with the optional parameter to the curry function that allows us to set the number of arguments of the function being curried.

```
var hexs = nums2hex.curry(2);
console.log(hexs(11)(12));       // returns 0b0c
console.log(hexs(11));           // returns function
console.log(hexs(110)(12)(0));   // incorrect
```

Therefore currying does not work well with functions that accept variable numbers of arguments. For something like that, partial application is preferred.

All of this isn't just for the benefit of function factories and code reuse. Currying and partial application play into a bigger pattern known as composition.

Function composition

Finally, we have arrived at function composition.

In functional programming, we want everything to be a function. We especially want unary functions if possible. If we can convert all functions to unary functions, then magical things can happen.

> **Unary** functions are functions that take only a single input. Functions with multiple inputs are **polyadic**, but we usually say *binary* for functions that accept two inputs and **ternary** for three inputs. Some functions don't accept a specific number of inputs; we call those **variadic**.

Manipulating functions and their acceptable number of inputs can be extremely expressive. In this section, we will explore how to compose new functions from smaller functions: little units of logic that combine into whole programs that are greater than the sum of the functions on their own.

Compose

Composing functions allows us to build complex functions from many simple, generic functions. By treating functions as building blocks for other functions, we can build truly modular applications with excellent readability and maintainability.

Before we define the `compose()` polyfill, you can see how it all works with these following examples:

```
var roundedSqrt = Math.round.compose(Math.sqrt)
console.log( roundedSqrt(5) ); // Returns: 2

var squaredDate =  roundedSqrt.compose(Date.parse)
console.log( squaredDate("January 1, 2014") ); // Returns: 1178370
```

In math, the composition of the `f` and `g` variables is defined as `f(g(x))`. In JavaScript, this can be written as:

```
var compose = function(f, g) {
  return function(x) {
    return f(g(x));
  };
};
```

But if we left it at that, we would lose track of the `this` keyword, among other problems. The solution is to use the `apply()` and `call()` utilities. Compared to curry, the `compose()` polyfill is quite simple.

```
Function.prototype.compose = function(prevFunc) {
  var nextFunc = this;
  return function() {
    return nextFunc.call(this,prevFunc.apply(this,arguments));
  }
}
```

To show how it's used, let's build a completely contrived example, as follows:

```
function function1(a){return a + ' 1';}
function function2(b){return b + ' 2';}
function function3(c){return c + ' 3';}
var composition = function3.compose(function2).compose(function1);
console.log( composition('count') ); // returns 'count 1 2 3'
```

Did you notice that the `function3` parameter was applied first? This is very important. Functions are applied from right to left.

Sequence – compose in reverse

Because many people like to read things from the left to the right, it might make sense to apply the functions in that order too. We'll call this a sequence instead of a composition.

To reverse the order, all we need to do is swap the `nextFunc` and `prevFunc` parameters.

```
Function.prototype.sequence = function(prevFunc) {
  var nextFunc = this;
  return function() {
    return prevFunc.call(this,nextFunc.apply(this,arguments));
  }
}
```

This allows us to now call the functions in a more natural order.

```
var sequences = function1.sequence(function2).sequence(function3);
console.log( sequences('count') ); // returns 'count 1 2 3'
```

Compositions versus chains

Here are five different implementations of the same `floorSqrt()` functional composition. They seem to be identical, but they deserve scrutiny.

```
function floorSqrt1(num) {
  var sqrtNum = Math.sqrt(num);
  var floorSqrt = Math.floor(sqrtNum);
  var stringNum = String(floorSqrt);
  return stringNum;
}

function floorSqrt2(num) {
  return String(Math.floor(Math.sqrt(num)));
}

function floorSqrt3(num) {
  return [num].map(Math.sqrt).map(Math.floor).toString();
}
var floorSqrt4 = String.compose(Math.floor).compose(Math.sqrt);
var floorSqrt5 = Math.sqrt.sequence(Math.floor).sequence(String);

// all functions can be called like this:
floorSqrt<N>(17); // Returns: 4
```

But there are a few key differences we should go over:

- Obviously the first method is verbose and inefficient.
- The second method is a nice one-liner, but this approach becomes very unreadable after only a few functions are applied.

To say that less code is better is missing the point. Code is more maintainable when the effective instructions are more concise. If you reduce the number of characters on the screen without changing the effective instructions carried out, this has the complete opposite effect—code becomes harder to understand, and decidedly less maintainable; for example, when we use nested ternary operators, or we chain several commands together on a single line. These approaches reduce the amount of 'code on the screen', but they don't reduce the number of steps actually being specified by that code. So the effect is to obfuscate and make the code harder to understand. The kind of conciseness that makes code easier to maintain is that which effectively reduces the specified instructions (for example, by using a simpler algorithm that accomplishes the same result with fewer and/ or simpler steps), or when we simply replace code with a message, for instance, invoking a third-party library with a well-documented API.

- The third approach is a chain of array functions, notably the `map` function. This works fairly well, but it is not mathematically correct.
- Here's our `compose()` function in action. All methods are forced to be unary, pure functions that encourage the use of better, simpler, and smaller functions that do one thing and do it well.
- The last approach uses the `compose()` function in reverse sequence, which is just as valid.

Programming with compose

The most important aspect of compose is that, aside from the first function that is applied, it works best with pure, *unary* functions: functions that take only one argument.

The output of the first function that is applied is sent to the next function. This means that the function must accept what the previous function passed to it. This is the main influence behind *type signatures*.

> Type Signatures are used to explicitly declare what types of input the function accepts and what type it outputs. They were first used by Haskell, which actually used them in the function definitions to be used by the compiler. But, in JavaScript, we just put them in a code comment. They look something like this: `foo :: arg1 -> argN -> output`
>
> Examples:
> ```
> // getStringLength :: String -> Int
> function getStringLength(s){return s.length};
> // concatDates :: Date -> Date -> [Date]
> function concatDates(d1,d2){return [d1, d2]};
> // pureFunc :: (int -> Bool) -> [int] -> [int]
> pureFunc(func, arr){return arr.filter(func)}
> ```

In order to truly reap the benefits of compose, any application will need a hefty collection of unary, pure functions. These are the building blocks that are composed into larger functions that, in turn, are used to make applications that are very modular, reliable, and maintainable.

Let's go through an example. First we'll need many building-block functions. Some of them build upon the others as follows:

```
// stringToArray :: String -> [Char]
function stringToArray(s) { return s.split(''); }

// arrayToString :: [Char] -> String
```

```
function arrayToString(a) { return a.join(''); }

// nextChar :: Char -> Char
function nextChar(c) {
  return String.fromCharCode(c.charCodeAt(0) + 1); }

// previousChar :: Char -> Char
function previousChar(c) {
  return String.fromCharCode(c.charCodeAt(0)-1); }

// higherColorHex :: Char -> Char
function higherColorHex(c) {return c >= 'f' ? 'f' :
                                    c == '9' ? 'a' :
                                    nextChar(c)}

// lowerColorHex :: Char -> Char
function lowerColorHex(c) { return c <= '0' ? '0' :
                                   c == 'a' ? '9' :
                                   previousChar(c); }

// raiseColorHexes :: String -> String
function raiseColorHexes(arr) { return arr.map(higherColorHex); }

// lowerColorHexes :: String -> String
function lowerColorHexes(arr) { return arr.map(lowerColorHex); }
```

Now let's compose some of them together.

```
var lighterColor = arrayToString
  .compose(raiseColorHexes)
  .compose(stringToArray)
  var darkerColor = arrayToString
  .compose(lowerColorHexes)
  .compose(stringToArray)

console.log( lighterColor('af0189') ); // Returns: 'bf129a'
console.log( darkerColor('af0189')  );  // Returns: '9e0078'
```

We can even use `compose()` and `curry()` functions together. In fact, they work very well together. Let's forge together the curry example with our compose example. First we'll need our helper functions from before.

```
// component2hex :: Ints -> Int
function componentToHex(c) {
  var hex = c.toString(16);
  return hex.length == 1 ? "0" + hex : hex;
```

```
}

// nums2hex :: Ints* -> Int
function nums2hex() {
  return Array.prototype.map.call(arguments,
  componentToHex).join('');
}
```

First we need to make the curried and partial-applied functions, then we can compose them to our other composed functions.

```
var lighterColors = lighterColor
  .compose(nums2hex.curry());
var darkerRed = darkerColor
  .compose(nums2hex.partialApply(255));
Var lighterRgb2hex = lighterColor
  .compose(nums2hex.partialApply());

console.log( lighterColors(123, 0, 22) ); // Returns: 8cff11
console.log( darkerRed(123, 0) ); // Returns: ee6a00
console.log( lighterRgb2hex(123,200,100) ); // Returns: 8cd975
```

There we have it! The functions read really well and make a lot of sense. We were forced to begin with little functions that just did one thing. Then we were able to put together functions with more utility.

Let's look at one last example. Here's a function that lightens an RBG value by a variable amount. Then we can use composition to create new functions from it.

```
// lighterColorNumSteps :: string -> num -> string
function lighterColorNumSteps(color, n) {
  for (var i = 0; i < n; i++) {
    color = lighterColor(color);
  }
  return color;
}

// now we can create functions like this:
var lighterRedNumSteps =
lighterColorNumSteps.curry().compose(reds)(0,0);

// and use them like this:
console.log( lighterRedNumSteps(5) ); // Return: 'ff5555'
console.log( lighterRedNumSteps(2) ); // Return: 'ff2222'
```

In the same way, we could easily create more functions for creating lighter and darker blues, greens, grays, purples, anything you want. *This is a really great way to construct an API.*

We just barely scratched the surface of what function composition can do. What compose does is take control away from JavaScript. Normally JavaScript will evaluate left to right, but now the interpreter is saying "OK, something else is going to take care of this, I'll just move on to the next." And now the `compose()` function has control over the evaluation sequence!

This is how `Lazy.js`, `Bacon.js` and others have been able to implement things such as lazy evaluation and infinite sequences. Up next, we'll look into how those libraries are used.

Mostly functional programming

What is a program without side effects? A program that does nothing.

Complementing our code with functional code with unavoidable side-effects can be called "mostly functional programming." Using multiple paradigms in the same codebase and applying them where they are most optimal is the best approach. Mostly functional programming is how even the pure, traditional functional programs are modelled: keep most of the logic in pure functions and interface with imperative code.

And this is how we're going to write a little application of our own.

In this example, we have a boss that tells us that we need a web application for our company that tracks the status of the employees' availability. All the employees at this fictional company only have one job: using our website. Staff will sign in when they get to work and sign out when they leave. But that's not enough, it also needs to automatically update the content as it changes, so our boss doesn't have to keep refreshing the pages.

We're going to use `Lazy.js` as our functional library. And we're also going to be lazy: instead of worrying about handling all the users logging in and out, WebSockets, databases, and more, we'll just pretend there's a generic application object that does this for us and just happens to have the perfect API.

So for now, let's just get the ugly parts out of the way, the parts that interface and create side-effects.

```
function Receptor(name, available){
  this.name = name;
  this.available = available; // mutable state
```

```
    this.render = function(){
      output = '<li>';
      output += this.available ?
        this.name + ' is available' :
        this.name + ' is not available';
      output += '</li>';
      return output;
    }
  }
  var me = new Receptor;
  var receptors = app.getReceptors().push(me);
  app.container.innerHTML = receptors.map(function(r){
    return r.render();
  }).join('');
```

This would be sufficient for just displaying a list of availabilities, but we want it to be reactive, which brings us to our first obstacle.

By using the `Lazy.js` library to store the objects in a sequence, which won't actually compute anything until the `toArray()` method is called, we can take advantage of its laziness to provide a sort of functional reactive programming.

```
  var lazyReceptors = Lazy(receptors).map(function(r){
    return r.render();
  });
  app.container.innerHTML = lazyReceptors.toArray().join('');
```

Because the `Receptor.render()` method returns new HTML instead of modifying the current HTML, all we have to do is set the `innerHTML` parameter to its output.

We'll also have to trust that our generic application for user management will provide callback methods for us to use.

```
  app.onUserLogin = function(){
    this.available = true;
    app.container.innerHTML = lazyReceptors.toArray().join('');
  };
  app.onUserLogout = function(){
    this.available = false;
    app.container.innerHTML = lazyReceptors.toArray().join('');
  };
```

This way, any time a user logs in or out, the `lazyReceptors` parameter will be computed again and the availability list will be printed with the most recent values.

Handling events

But what if the application doesn't provide callbacks for when the user logs in and out? Callbacks are messy and can quickly turn a program into spaghetti code. Instead, we can determine it ourselves by observing the user directly. If the user has the webpage in focus, then he/she must be active and available. We can use JavaScript's focus and blur events for this.

```
window.addEventListener('focus', function(event) {
  me.available = true;
  app.setReceptor(me.name, me.available); // just go with it
  container.innerHTML = lazyReceptors.toArray().join('');
});
window.addEventListener('blur', function(event) {
  me.available = false;
  app.setReceptor(me.name, me.available);
  container.innerHTML = lazyReceptors.toArray().join('');
});
```

Wait a second, aren't events reactive too? Can they be lazily computed as well? They can in the Lazy.js library, where there's even a handy method for this.

```
var focusedReceptors = Lazy.events(window,
"focus").each(function(e){
  me.available = true;
  app.setReceptor(me.name, me.available);
  container.innerHTML = lazyReceptors.toArray().join('');
});
var blurredReceptors = Lazy.events(window,
"blur").each(function(e){
  me.available = false;
  app.setReceptor(me.name, me.available);
  container.innerHTML = lazyReceptors.toArray().join('');
});
```

Easy as pie.

> By using the Lazy.js library to handle events, we can create an infinite sequence of events. Each time the event is fired, the Lazy.each() function is able to iterate one more time.

Our boss likes the application so far, but she points out that if an employee never logs out before leaving for the day without closing the page, then the application says the employee is still available.

To figure out if an employee is active on the website, we can monitor the keyboard and mouse events. Let's say they're considered to be unavailable after 30 minutes of no activity.

```
var timeout = null;
var inputs = Lazy.events(window, "mousemove").each(function(e){
  me.available = true;
  container.innerHTML = lazyReceptors.toArray().join('');
  clearTimeout(timeout);
  timeout = setTimeout(function(){
    me.available = false;
    container.innerHTML = lazyReceptors.toArray().join('');
  }, 1800000); // 30 minutes
});
```

The `Lazy.js` library has made it very easy for us to handle events as an infinite stream that we can map over. It makes this possible because it uses function composition to take control of the order of execution.

But there's a little problem with all of this. What if there are no user input events that we can latch onto? What if, instead, there is a property value that changes all the time? In the next section, we'll investigate exactly this issue.

Functional reactive programming

Let's build another kind of application that works in much the same way; one that uses functional programming to react to changes in state. But, this time, the application won't be able to rely on event listeners.

Imagine for a moment that you work for a news media company and your boss tells you to create a web application that tracks government election results on Election Day. Data is continuously flowing in as local precincts turn in their results, so the results to display on the page are very reactive. But we also need to track the results by each region, so there will be multiple objects to track.

Rather than creating a big object-oriented hierarchy to model the interface, we can describe it declaratively as immutable data. We can transform it with chains of pure and semi-pure functions whose only ultimate side effects are updating whatever bits of state absolutely must be held onto (ideally, not many).

And we'll use the `Bacon.js` library, which will allow us to quickly develop **Functional Reactive Programming (FRP)** applications. The application will only be used one day out of the year (Election Day), and our boss thinks it should take a proportional amount of time. With functional programming and a library such as `Bacon.js`, we'll get it done in half the time.

But first, we're going to need some objects to represent the voting regions, such as states, provinces, districts, and so on.

```
function Region(name, percent, parties){
  // mutable properties:
  this.name = name;
  this.percent = percent; // % of precincts reported
  this.parties = parties; // political parties

  // return an HTML representation
  this.render = function(){
    var lis = this.parties.map(function(p){
      return '<li>' + p.name + ': ' + p.votes + '</li>';
    });
    var output = '<h2>' + this.name + '</h2>';
    output += '<ul>' + lis.join('') + '</ul>';
    output += 'Percent reported: ' + this.percent;
    return output;
  }
}
function getRegions(data) {
  return JSON.parse(data).map(function(obj){
    return new Region(obj.name, obj.percent, obj.parties);
  });
}
var url = 'http://api.server.com/election-data?format=json';
var data = jQuery.ajax(url);
var regions = getRegions(data);
app.container.innerHTML = regions.map(function(r){
  return r.render();
}).join('');
```

While the above would be sufficient for just displaying a static list of election results, we need a way to update the regions dynamically. It's time to cook up some Bacon and FRP.

Reactivity

Bacon has a function, `Bacon.fromPoll()`, that lets us create an event stream, where the event is just a function that is called on the given interval. And the `stream.subscribe()` function lets us *subscribe* a handler function to the stream. Because it's lazy, the stream will not actually do anything without a subscriber.

```
var eventStream = Bacon.fromPoll(10000, function(){
  return Bacon.Next;
});
var subscriber = eventStream.subscribe(function(){
  var url = 'http://api.server.com/election-data?format=json';
```

```
    var data = jQuery.ajax(url);
    var newRegions = getRegions(data);
    container.innerHTML = newRegions.map(function(r){
      return r.render();
    }).join('');
  });
```

By essentially putting it in a loop that runs every 10 seconds, we could get the job done. But this method would hammer-ping the network and is incredibly inefficient. That would not be very functional. Instead, let's dig a little deeper into the `Bacon.js` library.

In Bacon, there are EventStreams and Properties parameters. Properties can be thought of as "magic" variables that change over time in response to events. They're not really magic because they still rely on a stream of events. The Property changes over time in relation to its EventStream.

The `Bacon.js` library has another trick up its sleeve. The `Bacon.fromPromise()` function is a way to emit events into a stream by using *promises*. And as of jQuery version 1.5.0, jQuery AJAX implements the promises interface. So all we need to do is write an AJAX search function that emits events when the asynchronous call is complete. Every time the promise is resolved, it calls the EvenStream's subscribers.

```
  var url = 'http://api.server.com/election-data?format=json';
  var eventStream = Bacon.fromPromise(jQuery.ajax(url));
  var subscriber = eventStream.onValue(function(data){
    newRegions = getRegions(data);
    container.innerHTML = newRegions.map(function(r){
      return r.render();
    }).join('');
  }
```

A promise can be thought of as an *eventual value*; with the `Bacon.js` library, we can lazily wait on the eventual values.

Putting it all together

Now that we have the reactivity covered, we can finally play with some code.

We can modify the subscriber with chains of pure functions to do things such as adding up a total and filtering out unwanted results, and we do it all within `onclick()` handler functions for buttons that we create.

```
  // create the eventStream out side of the functions
  var eventStream = Bacon.onPromise(jQuery.ajax(url));
  var subscribe = null;
```

```javascript
var url = 'http://api.server.com/election-data?format=json';

// our un-modified subscriber
$('button#showAll').click(function() {
  var subscriber = eventStream.onValue(function(data) {
    var newRegions = getRegions(data).map(function(r) {
      return new Region(r.name, r.percent, r.parties);
    });
    container.innerHTML = newRegions.map(function(r) {
      return r.render();
    }).join('');
  });
});

// a button for showing the total votes
$('button#showTotal').click(function() {
  var subscriber = eventStream.onValue(function(data) {
    var emptyRegion = new Region('empty', 0, [{
      name: 'Republican', votes: 0
    }, {
      name: 'Democrat', votes: 0
    }]);
    var totalRegions = getRegions(data).reduce(function(r1, r2) {
      newParties = r1.parties.map(function(x, i) {
      return {
        name: r1.parties[i].name,
        votes: r1.parties[i].votes + r2.parties[i].votes
      };
    });
    newRegion = new Region('Total', (r1.percent + r2.percent) / 2,
    newParties);
    return newRegion;
    }, emptyRegion);
    container.innerHTML = totalRegions.render();
  });
});

// a button for only displaying regions that are reporting > 50%
$('button#showMostlyReported').click(function() {
  var subscriber = eventStream.onValue(function(data) {
    var newRegions = getRegions(data).map(function(r) {
      if (r.percent > 50) return r;
      else return null;
    }).filter(function(r) {return r != null;});
```

```
      container.innerHTML = newRegions.map(function(r) {
        return r.render();
      }).join('');
    });
  });
```

The beauty of this is that, when users click between the buttons, the event stream doesn't change but the subscriber does, which makes it all work smoothly.

Summary

JavaScript is a beautiful language.

Its inner beauty really shines with functional programming. It's what empowers its excellent extendibility. Just the fact that it allows first-class functions that can do so many things is what opens the functional flood gates. Concepts build on top of each other, stacking up higher and higher.

In this chapter, we dove head-first into the functional paradigm in JavaScript. We covered function factories, currying, function composition and everything required to make it work. We built an extremely modular application that used these concepts. And then we showed how to use some functional libraries that use these same concepts themselves, namely function composition, to manipulate the order of execution.

Throughout the chapter, we covered several styles of functional programming: data generic programming, mostly-functional programming, and functional reactive programming. They're all not that different from each other, they're just different patterns for applying functional programing in different situations.

In the previous chapter, something called Category Theory was briefly mentioned. In the next chapter, we're going to learn a lot more about what it is and how to use it.

5
Category Theory

Thomas Watson was famously quoted as saying, "I think there is a world market for maybe five computers". That was in 1948. Back then, everybody knew that computers would only be used for two things: math and engineering. Not even the biggest minds in tech could predict that, one day, computers would be able to translate Spanish to English, or simulate entire weather systems. At the time, the fastest machine was IBM's SSEC, clocking in at 50 multiplications per second, the display terminal wasn't due until 15 years later and multiple-processing meant multiple user terminals sharing a single processor. The transistor changed everything, but tech's visionaries still missed the mark. Ken Olson made another famously foolish prediction when, in 1977, he said "There is no reason anyone would want a computer in their home".

It seams obvious to us now that computers are not just for scientists and engineers, but that's hindsight. The idea that machines can do more than just math was anything but intuitive 70 years ago. Watson didn't just fail to realize how computers could transform a society, he failed to realize the transformative and evolving powers of mathematics.

But the potential of computers and math was not lost on everybody. John McCarthy invented **Lisp** in 1958, a revolutionary algorithm-based language that ushered in a new era in computing. Since its inception, Lisp was instrumental in the idea of using abstraction layers—compilers, interpreters, virtualization—to push forward the progression of computers from hardcore math machines to what they are today.

From Lisp came **Scheme**, a direct ancestor of JavaScript. Now that brings us full circle. If computers are, at their core, machines that just do math, then it stands to reason that a math-based programming paradigm would excel.

The term "math" is being used here not to describe the "number crunching" that computers can obviously do, but to describe *discrete mathematics*: the study of discrete, mathematical structures such as statements in logic or the instructions of a computer language. By treating code as a discrete mathematical structure, we can apply concepts and ideas in math to it. This is what has made functional programming so instrumental in artificial intelligence, graph search, pattern recognition and other big challenges in computer science.

In this chapter, we will experiment with some of these concepts and their applications in everyday programming challenges. They will include:

- Category theory
- Morphisms
- Functors
- Maybes
- Promises
- Lenses
- Function composition

With these concepts, we'll be able to write entire libraries and APIs very easily and safely. And we'll go from explaining category theory to formally implementing it in JavaScript.

Category theory

Category theory is the theoretical concept that empowers function composition. Category theory and function composition go together like engine displacement and horsepower, like NASA and the space shuttle, like good beer and a mug to pour it in. Basically, you can't have one without the other.

Category theory in a nutshell

Category theory really isn't too difficult a concept. Its place in math is large enough to fill up an entire graduate-level college course, but its place in computer programming can be summed up quite easily.

Einstein once said, "If you can't explain it to a 6-year-old, you don't know it yourself". Thus, in the spirit of explaining it to a 6-year-old, *category theory is just connecting the dots*. Although it may be grossly over-simplifying category theory, it does do a good job of explaining what we need to know in a straightforward manner.

First you'll need to know some terminology. **Categories** are just sets with the same type. In JavaScript, they're arrays or objects that contain variables that are explicitly declared as numbers, strings, Booleans, dates, nodes, and so on. **Morphisms** are pure functions that, when given a specific set of inputs, always return the same output. **Homomorphic operations** are restricted to a single category, while **polymorphic operations** can operate on multiple categories. For example, the homomorphic function *multiplication* only works on numbers, but the polymorphic function addition can work on strings too.

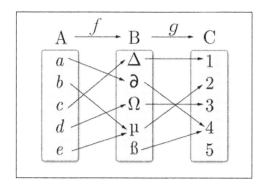

The following diagram shows three categories—A, B, and C—and two morphisms—*f* and ⬚.

Category theory tells us that, when we have two morphisms where the category of the first one is the expected input of the other, then they can be *composed* to the following:

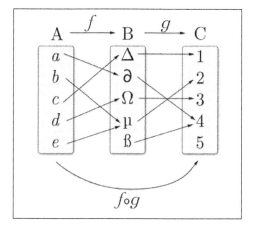

The *f o g* symbol is the composition of morphisms *f* and *g*. Now we can just connect the dots.

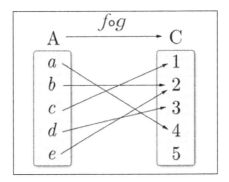

And that's all it really is, just connecting dots.

Type safety

Let's connect some dots. Categories contain two things:

1. Objects (in JavaScript, types).
2. Morphisms (in JavaScript, pure functions that only work on types).

These are the terms given to category theory by mathematicians, so there is some unfortunate nomenclature overloading with our JavaScript terminology. **Objects** in category theory are more like variables with an explicit data type and not collections of properties and values like in the JavaScript definition of objects. **Morphisms** are just pure functions that use those types.

So applying the idea of category theory to JavaScript is pretty easy. Using category theory in JavaScript means working with one certain data type per category. Data types are numbers, strings, arrays, dates, objects, Booleans, and so on. But, with no strict type system in JavaScript, things can go awry. So we'll have to implement our own method of ensuring that the data is correct.

There are four primitive data types in JavaScript: numbers, strings, Booleans, and functions. We can create *type safety functions* that either return the variable or throw an error. *This fulfils the object axiom of categories.*

```
var str = function(s) {
  if (typeof s === "string") {
    return s;
  }
}
```

```
      else {
        throw new TypeError("Error: String expected, " + typeof s + "
        given.");
      }
    }
    var num = function(n) {
      if (typeof n === "number") {
        return n;
      }
      else {
        throw new TypeError("Error: Number expected, " + typeof n + "
        given.");
      }
    }
    var bool = function(b) {
      if (typeof b === "boolean") {
        return b;
      }
      else {
        throw new TypeError("Error: Boolean expected, " + typeof b + "
        given.");
      }
    }
    var func = function(f) {
      if (typeof f === "function") {
        return f;
      }
      else {
        throw new TypeError("Error: Function expected, " + typeof f +
        " given.");
      }
    }
```

However, there's a lot of repeated code here and that isn't very functional. Instead, we can create a function that returns another function that is the type safety function.

```
    var typeOf = function(type) {
      return function(x) {
        if (typeof x === type) {
          return x;
        }
        else {
          throw new TypeError("Error: "+type+" expected, "+typeof x+"
          given.");
        }
```

```
    }
  }
  var str = typeOf('string'),
    num = typeOf('number'),
    func = typeOf('function'),
    bool = typeOf('boolean');
```

Now, we can use them to ensure that our functions behave as expected.

```
// unprotected method:
var x = '24';
x + 1; // will return '241', not 25

// protected method
// plusplus :: Int -> Int
function plusplus(n) {
  return num(n) + 1;
}
plusplus(x); // throws error, preferred over unexpected output
```

Let's look at a meatier example. If we want to check the length of a Unix timestamp that is returned by the JavaScript function Date.parse(), not as a string but as a number, then we'll have to use our str() function.

```
// timestampLength :: String -> Int
function timestampLength(t) { return num(str(t).length); }
timestampLength(Date.parse('12/31/1999')); // throws error
timestampLength(Date.parse('12/31/1999')
   .toString()); // returns 12
```

Functions like this that explicitly transform one type to another (or to the same type) are called *morphisms*. *This fulfils the morphism axiom of category theory.* These forced type declarations via the type safety functions and the morphisms that use them are everything we need to represent the notion of a category in JavaScript.

Object identities

There's one other important data type: objects.

```
var obj = typeOf('object');
obj(123); // throws error
obj({x:'a'}); // returns {x:'a'}
```

However, objects are different. They can be inherited. Everything that is not a primitive—numbers, strings, Booleans, and functions—is an object, including arrays, dates, elements, and more.

There's no way to know what type of object something is, as in to know what sub-type a JavaScript 'object' is, from the `typeof` keyword, so we'll have to improvise. Objects have a `toString()` function that we can hijack for this purpose.

```
var obj = function(o) {
  if (Object.prototype.toString.call(o)==="[object Object]") {
    return o;
  }
  else {
    throw new TypeError("Error: Object expected, something else
    given.");
  }
}
```

Again, with all the objects out there, we should implement some code re-use.

```
var objectTypeOf = function(name) {
  return function(o) {
    if (Object.prototype.toString.call(o) === "[object "+name+"]")
    {
      return o;
    }
    else {
      throw new TypeError("Error: '+name+' expected, something
      else given.");
    }
  }
}
var obj = objectTypeOf('Object');
var arr = objectTypeOf('Array');
var date = objectTypeOf('Date');
var div = objectTypeOf('HTMLDivElement');
```

These will be very useful for our next topic: functors.

Functors

While morphisms are mappings between types, *functors* are mappings between categories. They can be thought of as functions that lift values out of a container, morph them, and then put them into a new container. The first input is a morphism for the type and the second input is the container.

> The type signature for functors looks like this:
>
>   // myFunctor :: (a -> b) -> f a -> f b
>
> This says, "give me a function that takes a and returns b and a box that contains a(s), and I'll return a box that contains b(s).

Creating functors

It turns out we already have one functor: `map()`. It grabs the values within the container, an array, and applies a function to it.

```
[1, 4, 9].map(Math.sqrt); // Returns: [1, 2, 3]
```

However, we'll need to write it as a global function and not as a method of the array object. This will allow us to write cleaner, safer code later on.

```
// map :: (a -> b) -> [a] -> [b]
var map = function(f, a) {
  return arr(a).map(func(f));
}
```

This example seems like a contrived wrapper because we're just piggybacking onto the `map()` function. But it serves a purpose. It provides a template for maps of other types.

```
// strmap :: (str -> str) -> str -> str
var strmap = function(f, s) {
  return str(s).split('').map(func(f)).join('');
}

// MyObject#map :: (myValue -> a) -> a
MyObject.prototype.map(f{
  return func(f)(this.myValue);
}
```

Arrays and functors

Arrays are the preferred way to work with data in functional JavaScript.

Is there an easier way to create functors that are already assigned to a morphism? Yes, and it's called `arrayOf`. When you pass in a morphism that expects an integer and returns an array, you get back a morphism that expects an array of integers and returns an array of arrays.

It is not a functor itself, but it allows us to create functors from morphisms.

```
// arrayOf :: (a -> b) -> ([a] -> [b])
var arrayOf = function(f) {
  return function(a) {
    return map(func(f), arr(a));
  }
}
```

Here's how to create functors by using morphism:

```
var plusplusall = arrayOf(plusplus); // plusplus is our morphism
console.log( plusplusall([1,2,3]) ); // returns [2,3,4]
console.log( plusplusall([1,'2',3]) ); // error is thrown
```

The interesting property of the `arrayOf` functor is that it works on type safeties as well. When you pass in the type safety function for strings, you get back a type safety function for an array of strings. The type safeties are treated like the *identity function* morphism. This can be very useful for ensuring that an array contains all the correct types.

```
var strs = arrayOf(str);
console.log( strs(['a','b','c']) ); // returns ['a','b','c']
console.log( strs(['a',2,'c']) ); // throws error
```

Function compositions, revisited

Functions are another type of primitive that we can create a functor for. And that functor is called `fcompose`. We defined functors as something that takes a value from a container and applies a function to it. When that container is a function, we just call it to get its inner value.

We already know what function compositions are, but let's look at what they can do in a category theory-driven environment.

Function compositions are associative. If your high school algebra teacher was like mine, she taught you what the property *is* but not what it can *do*. In practice, compose is what the associative property can do.

$$(a \times b) \times c = a \times (b \times c)$$
$$(f \circ g) \circ h = f \circ (g \circ h)$$

$$f \circ g \neq g \circ f$$

Category Theory

We can do any inner-compose, it doesn't matter how it's grouped. This is not to be confused with the commutative property. *f o g* does not always equal *g o f*. In other words, the reverse of the first word of a string is not the same as the first word of the reverse of a string.

What this all means is that it doesn't matter which functions are applied and in what order, as long as the input of each functions comes from the output of the previous function. But wait, if the function on the right relies on the function on the left, then can't there be only one order of evaluation? Left to right? True, but if it's encapsulated, then we can control it however we feel fit. This is what empowered lazy evaluation in JavaScript.

$$(a \times b) \times c = a \times (b \times c)$$
$$(f \circ g) \circ h = f \circ (g \circ h)$$

Let's rewrite function composition, not as an extension of the function prototype, but as a stand-alone function that will allow us to get more out of it. The basic form is as follows:

```
var fcompose = function(f, g) {
  return function() {
    return f.call(this, g.apply(this, arguments));
  };
};
```

But we'll need it to work on any number of inputs.

```
var fcompose = function() {
  // first make sure all arguments are functions
  var funcs = arrayOf(func)(arguments);

  // return a function that applies all the functions
  return function() {
    var argsOfFuncs = arguments;
    for (var i = funcs.length; i > 0; i -= 1) {
      argsOfFuncs = [funcs[i].apply(this, args)];
    }
    return args[0];
  };
};

// example:
```

```
var f = fcompose(negate, square, mult2, add1);
f(2); // Returns: -36
```

Now that we've encapsulated the functions, we have control over them. We could rewrite the compose function such that *each function accepts another function as input, stores it, and gives back an object that does the same*. Instead of accepting an array as an input, doing something with it, and then giving back a new array for each operation, we can accept a single array for each element in the source, perform all operations combined (every `map()`, `filter()`, and so on, composed together), and finally store the results in a new array. This is lazy evaluation via function composition. No reason to reinvent the wheel here. Many libraries have a nice implementation of this concept, including the `Lazy.js`, `Bacon.js` and `wu.js` libraries.

There's a lot more we can do as a result of this different model: asynchronous iteration, asynchronous event handling, lazy evaluation, and even automatic parallelization.

Automatic parallelization? There's a word for that in the computer science industry: IMPOSSIBLE. But is it really impossible? The next evolutionary leap in Moore's law might be a compiler that parallelizes our code for us, and could function composition be it?

No, it doesn't quite work that way. The JavaScript engine is what is really doing the parallelization, not automatically but with well thought-out code. Compose just gives the engine the chance to split it into parallel processes. But that in itself is pretty cool.

Monads

Monads are tools that help you compose functions.

Like primitive types, monads are structures that can be used as the containers that functors "reach into". The functors grab the data, do something to it, put it into a new monad, and return it.

There are three monads we'll focus on:

- Maybes
- Promises
- Lenses

So in addition to arrays (map) and functions (compose), we'll have five functors (map, compose, maybe, promise and lens). These are just some of the many other functors and monads that are out there.

Maybes

Maybes allow us to gracefully work with data that might be null and to have defaults. A maybe is a variable that either has some value or it doesn't. And it doesn't matter to the caller.

On its own, it might seem like this is not that big a deal. Everybody knows that null-checks are easily accomplished with an `if-else` statement:

```
if (getUsername() == null ) {
  username = 'Anonymous') {
else {
  username = getUsername();
}
```

But with functional programming, we're breaking away from the procedural, line-by-line way of doing things and instead working with pipelines of functions and data. If we had to break the chain in the middle just to check if the value existed or not, we would have to create temporary variables and write more code. Maybes are just tools to help us keep the logic flowing through the pipeline.

To implement maybes, we'll first need to create some constructors.

```
// the Maybe monad constructor, empty for now
var Maybe = function(){};

// the None instance, a wrapper for an object with no value
var None = function(){};
None.prototype = Object.create(Maybe.prototype);
None.prototype.toString = function(){return 'None';};

// now we can write the `none` function
// saves us from having to write `new None()` all the time
var none = function(){return new None()};

// and the Just instance, a wrapper for an object with a value
var Just = function(x){return this.x = x;};
Just.prototype = Object.create(Maybe.prototype);
Just.prototype.toString = function(){return "Just "+this.x;};
var just = function(x) {return new Just(x)};
```

Finally, we can write the `maybe` function. It returns a new function that either returns nothing or a maybe. *It is a functor.*

```
var maybe = function(m){
  if (m instanceof None) {
```

```
      return m;
    }
    else if (m instanceof Just) {
      return just(m.x);
    }
    else {
      throw new TypeError("Error: Just or None expected, " +
      m.toString() + " given.");
    }
  }
```

And we can also create a functor generator just like we did with arrays.

```
  var maybeOf = function(f){
    return function(m) {
      if (m instanceof None) {
        return m;
      }
      else if (m instanceof Just) {
        return just(f(m.x));
      }
      else {
        throw new TypeError("Error: Just or None expected, " +
        m.toString() + " given.");
      }
    }
  }
```

So `Maybe` is a monad, `maybe` is a functor, and `maybeOf` returns a functor that is already assigned to a morphism.

We'll need one more thing before we can move forward. We'll need to add a method to the `Maybe` monad object that helps us use it more intuitively.

```
  Maybe.prototype.orElse = function(y) {
    if (this instanceof Just) {
      return this.x;
    }
    else {
      return y;
    }
  }
```

Category Theory

In its raw form, maybes can be used directly.

```
maybe(just(123)).x; // Returns 123
maybeOf(plusplus)(just(123)).x; // Returns 124
maybe(plusplus)(none()).orElse('none'); // returns 'none'
```

Anything that returns a method that is then executed is complicated enough to be begging for trouble. So we can make it a little cleaner by calling on our `curry()` function.

```
maybePlusPlus = maybeOf.curry()(plusplus);
maybePlusPlus(just(123)).x; // returns 123
maybePlusPlus(none()).orElse('none'); // returns none
```

But the real power of maybes will become clear when the dirty business of directly calling the `none()` and `just()` functions is abstracted. We'll do this with an example object `User`, that uses maybes for the username.

```
var User = function(){
  this.username = none(); // initially set to `none`
};
User.prototype.setUsername = function(name) {
  this.username = just(str(name)); // it's now a `just
};
User.prototype.getUsernameMaybe = function() {
  var usernameMaybe = maybeOf.curry()(str);
  return usernameMaybe(this.username).orElse('anonymous');
};

var user = new User();
user.getUsernameMaybe(); // Returns 'anonymous'

user.setUsername('Laura');
user.getUsernameMaybe(); // Returns 'Laura'
```

And now we have a powerful and safe way to define defaults. Keep this `User` object in mind because we'll be using it later on in this chapter.

Promises

The nature of promises is that they remain immune to changing circumstances.
- Frank Underwood, House of Cards

In functional programming, we're often working with pipelines and data flows: chains of functions where each function produces a data type that is consumed by the next. However, many of these functions are asynchronous: readFile, events, AJAX, and so on. Instead of using a continuation-passing style and deeply nested callbacks, how can we modify the return types of these functions to indicate the result? By wrapping them in *promises*.

Promises are like the functional equivalent of callbacks. Obviously, callbacks are not all that functional because, if more than one function is mutating the same data, then there can be race conditions and bugs. Promises solve that problem.

You should use promises to turn this:

```
fs.readFile("file.json", function(err, val) {
  if( err ) {
    console.error("unable to read file");
  }
  else {
    try {
      val = JSON.parse(val);
      console.log(val.success);
    }
    catch( e ) {
      console.error("invalid json in file");
    }
  }
});
```

Into the following code snippet:

```
fs.readFileAsync("file.json").then(JSON.parse)
  .then(function(val) {
    console.log(val.success);
  })
  .catch(SyntaxError, function(e) {
    console.error("invalid json in file");
  })
  .catch(function(e){
    console.error("unable to read file")
  });
```

The preceding code is from the README for *bluebird*: a full featured *Promises/A+* implementation with exceptionally good performance. *Promises/A+* is a specification for implementing promises in JavaScript. Given its current debate within the JavaScript community, we'll leave the implementations up to the *Promises/A+* team, as it is much more complex than maybes.

But here's a partial implementation:

```
// the Promise monad
var Promise = require('bluebird');

// the promise functor
var promise = function(fn, receiver) {
  return function() {
    var slice = Array.prototype.slice,
    args = slice.call(arguments, 0, fn.length - 1),
    promise = new Promise();
    args.push(function() {
      var results = slice.call(arguments),
      error = results.shift();
      if (error) promise.reject(error);
      else promise.resolve.apply(promise, results);
    });
    fn.apply(receiver, args);
    return promise;
  };
};
```

Now we can use the `promise()` functor to transform functions that take callbacks into functions that return promises.

```
var files = ['a.json', 'b.json', 'c.json'];
readFileAsync = promise(fs.readFile);
var data = files
  .map(function(f){
    readFileAsync(f).then(JSON.parse)
  })
  .reduce(function(a,b){
    return $.extend({}, a, b)
  });
```

Lenses

Another reason why programmers really like monads is that they make writing libraries very easy. To explore this, let's extend our `User` object with more functions for getting and setting values but, instead of using getters and setters, we'll use *lenses*.

Lenses are first-class getters and setters. They allow us to not just get and set variables, but also to run functions over it. But instead of mutating the data, they clone and return the new data modified by the function. They force data to be immutable, which is great for security and consistency as well for libraries. They're great for elegant code no matter what the application, so long as the performance-hit of introducing additional array copies is not a critical issue.

Before we write the `lens()` function, let's look at how it works.

```
var first = lens(
  function (a) { return arr(a)[0]; }, // get
  function (a, b) { return [b].concat(arr(a).slice(1)); } // set
);
first([1, 2, 3]); // outputs 1
first.set([1, 2, 3], 5); // outputs [5, 2, 3]
function tenTimes(x) { return x * 10 }
first.modify(tenTimes, [1,2,3]); // outputs [10,2,3]
```

And here's how the `lens()` function works. It returns a function with get, set and mod defined. The `lens()` function itself is a functor.

```
var lens = fuction(get, set) {
  var f = function (a) {return get(a)};
  f.get = function (a) {return get(a)};
  f.set = set;
  f.mod = function (f, a) {return set(a, f(get(a)))};
  return f;
};
```

Let's try an example. We'll extend our `User` object from the previous example.

```
// userName :: User -> str
var userName = lens(
  function (u) {return u.getUsernameMaybe()}, // get
  function (u, v) { // set
    u.setUsername(v);
    return u.getUsernameMaybe();
  }
);

var bob = new User();
bob.setUsername('Bob');
userName.get(bob); // returns 'Bob'
userName.set(bob, 'Bobby'); //return 'Bobby'
userName.get(bob); // returns 'Bobby'
userName.mod(strToUpper, bob); // returns 'BOBBY'
strToUpper.compose(userName.set)(bob, 'robert'); // returns
'ROBERT'
userName.get(bob); // returns 'robert'
```

Category Theory

jQuery is a monad

If you think all this abstract babble about categories, functors, and monads has no real-world application, think again. jQuery, the popular JavaScript library that provides an enhanced interface for working with HTML is, in-fact, a monadic library.

The `jQuery` object is a monad and its methods are functors. Really, they're a special type of functor called *endofunctors*. **Endofunctors** are functors that return the same category as the input, that is, `F :: X -> X`. Each `jQuery` method takes a `jQuery` object and returns a `jQuery` object, which allows methods to be chained, and they will have the type signature `jFunc :: jquery-obj -> jquery-obj`.

```
$('li').add('p.me-too').css('color', 'red').attr({id:'foo'});
```

This is also what empowers jQuery's plugin framework. If the plugin takes a `jQuery` object as input and returns one as output, then it can be inserted into the chain.

Let's look at how jQuery was able to implement this.

Monads are the containers that the functors "reach into" to get the data. In this way, the data can be protected and controlled by the library. jQuery provides access to the underlying data, a wrapped set of HTML elements, via its many methods.

The `jQuery` object itself is written as the result of an anonymous function call.

```
var jQuery = (function () {
  var j = function (selector, context) {
    var jq-obj = new j.fn.init(selector, context);
    return jq-obj;
  };

  j.fn = j.prototype = {
    init: function (selector, context) {
      if (!selector) {
        return this;
      }
    }
  };
  j.fn.init.prototype = j.fn;
  return j;
})();
```

In this highly simplified version of jQuery, it returns a function that defines the `j` object, which is actually just an enhanced `init` constructor.

```
var $ = jQuery(); // the function is returned and assigned to `$`
var x = $('#select-me'); // jQuery object is returned
```

In the same way that functors lift values out of a container, jQuery wraps the HTML elements and provides access to them as opposed to modifying the HTML elements directly.

jQuery doesn't advertise this often, but it has its own `map()` method for lifting the HTML element objects out of the wrapper. Just like the `fmap()` method, the elements are lifted, something is done with them, and then they're placed back into the container. This is how many of jQuery's commands work in the backend.

```
$('li').map(function(index, element) {
  // do something to the element
  return element
});
```

Another library for working with HTML elements, Prototype, does not work like this. Prototype alters the HTML elements directly via helpers. Consequently, it has not faired as well in the JavaScript community.

Implementing categories

It's about time we formally defined category theory as JavaScript objects. Categories are objects (types) and morphisms (functions that only work on those types). It's an extremely high-level, totally-declarative way to program, but it ensures that the code is extremely safe and reliable—perfect for APIs and libraries that are worried about concurrency and type safety.

First, we'll need a function that helps us create morphisms. We'll call it `homoMorph()` because they'll be homomorphisms. It will return a function that expects a function to be passed in and produces the composition of it, based on the inputs. The inputs are the types that the morphism accepts as input and gives as output. Just like our type signatures, that is, `// morph :: num -> num -> [num]`, only the last one is the output.

```
var homoMorph = function( /* input1, input2,..., inputN, output */
) {
  var before =
  checkTypes(arrayOf(func)(Array.prototype.slice.call(arguments,
  0, arguments.length-1)));
```

Category Theory

```
      var after = func(arguments[arguments.length-1])
      return function(middle) {
        return function(args) {
          return after(middle.apply(this, before
          ([].slice.apply(arguments))));
        }
      }
    }

    // now we don't need to add type signature comments
    // because now they're built right into the function declaration
    add = homoMorph(num, num, num)(function(a,b){return a+b})
    add(12,24); // returns 36
    add('a', 'b'); // throws error
    homoMorph(num, num, num)(function(a,b){
      return a+b;
    })(18, 24); // returns 42
```

The `homoMorph()` function is fairly complex. It uses a closure (see *Chapter 2, Fundamentals of Functional Programming*) to return a function that accepts a function and checks its input and output values for type safety. And for that, it relies on a helper function: `checkTypes`, which is defined as follows:

```
    var checkTypes = function( typeSafeties ) {
      arrayOf(func)(arr(typeSafeties));
      var argLength = typeSafeties.length;
      return function(args) {
        arr(args);
        if (args.length != argLength) {
          throw new TypeError('Expected '+ argLength + ' arguments');
        }
        var results = [];
        for (var i=0; i<argLength; i++) {
          results[i] = typeSafeties[i](args[i]);
        }
        return results;
      }
    }
```

Now let's formally define some homomorphisms.

```
    var lensHM = homoMorph(func, func, func)(lens);
    var userNameHM = lensHM(
      function (u) {return u.getUsernameMaybe()}, // get
      function (u, v) { ·// set
```

```
      u.setUsername(v);
      return u.getUsernameMaybe();
    }
  )
  var strToUpperCase = homoMorph(str, str)(function(s) {
    return s.toUpperCase();
  });
  var morphFirstLetter = homoMorph(func, str, str)(function(f, s) {
    return f(s[0]).concat(s.slice(1));
  });
  var capFirstLetter = homoMorph(str, str)(function(s) {
    return morphFirstLetter(strToUpperCase, s)
  });
```

Finally, we can bring it on home. The following example includes function composition, lenses, homomorphisms, and more.

```
// homomorphic lenses
var bill = new User();
userNameHM.set(bill, 'William'); // Returns: 'William'
userNameHM.get(bill); // Returns: 'William'

// compose
var capatolizedUsername = fcompose(capFirstLetter,userNameHM.get);
capatolizedUsername(bill, 'bill'); // Returns: 'Bill'

// it's a good idea to use homoMorph on .set and .get too
var getUserName = homoMorph(obj, str)(userNameHM.get);
var setUserName = homoMorph(obj, str, str)(userNameHM.set);
getUserName(bill); // Returns: 'Bill'
setUserName(bill, 'Billy'); // Returns: 'Billy'

// now we can rewrite capatolizeUsername with the new setter
capatolizedUsername = fcompose(capFirstLetter, setUserName);
capatolizedUsername(bill, 'will'); // Returns: 'Will'
getUserName(bill); // Returns: 'will'
```

The preceding code is extremely declarative, safe, reliable, and dependable.

> What does it mean for code to be declarative? In imperative programming, we write sequences of instructions that tell the machine how to do what we want. In functional programming, we describe relationships between values that tell the machine what we want it to compute, and the machine figures out the instruction sequences to make it happen. Functional programming is declarative.

Entire libraries and APIs can be constructed this way that allow programmers to write code freely without worrying about concurrency and type safety because those worries are handled in the backend.

Summary

About one in every 2,000 people has a condition known as synesthesia, a neurological phenomenon in which one sensory input bleeds into another. The most common form involves assigning colors with letters. However, there is an even rarer form where sentences and paragraphs are associated with tastes and feelings.

For these people, they don't read word by word, sentence by sentence. They look at the whole page/document/program and get a sense for how it *tastes* — not in the mouth but in the *mind*. Then they put the parts of the text together like the pieces of a puzzle.

This is what it is like to write fully declarative code: code that describes the relationships between values that tells the machine what we want it to compute. The parts of the program are not instructions in line-by-line order. Synesthetics may be able to do it naturally, but with a little practice anyone can learn how to put the relational puzzle pieces together.

In this chapter, we looked at several mathematical concepts that apply to functional programming and how they allow us to build relationships between data. Next, we'll explore recursion and other advanced topics in JavaScript.

6
Advanced Topics and Pitfalls in JavaScript

JavaScript has been called the "assembly language of the web". The analogy (it isn't perfect, but which analogy is?) draws from the fact that JavaScipt is often a target for compilation, namely from **Clojure** and **CoffeeScript**, but also from many other sources such as **pyjamas** (python to JS) and Google Web Kit (Java to JS).

But the analogy also references the foolish idea that JavaScript is as expressive and low-level as x86 assembly. Perhaps this notion stems from the fact that JavaScript has been bashed for its design flaws and oversights ever since it was first shipped with Netscape back in 1995. It was developed and released in a hurry, before it could be fully developed. And because of that, some questionable design choices made its way into JavaScript, the language that soon became the de-facto scripting language of the web. Semicolons were a big mistake. So were its ambiguous methods for defining functions. Is it `var foo = function();` or `function foo();`?

Functional programming is an excellent way to side-step some of these mistakes. By focusing on the fact that JavaScript is truly a functional language, it becomes clear that, in the preceding example about the different ways to declare a function, it's best to declare functions as variables. And that semicolons are mostly just syntactic sugar to make JavaScript appear more C-like.

But always remember the language you are working with. JavaScript, like any other language, has its pitfalls. And, when programming in a style that often skirts the bleeding edge of what's possible, those minor stumbles can become non-recoverable gotchas. Some of these gotchas include:

- Recursion
- Variable scope and closures
- Function declarations vs. function expressions

However, these issues can be overcome with a little attention.

Recursion

Recursion is very important to functional programming in any language. Many functional languages go so far as to require recursion for iteration by not providing `for` and `while` loop statements; this is only possible when tail-call elimination is guaranteed by the language, which is not the case for JavaScript. A quick primer on recursion was given in *Chapter 2, Fundamentals of Functional Programming*. But in this section, we'll dig deeper into exactly how recursion works in JavaScript.

Tail recursion

JavaScript's routine for handling recursion is known as *tail recursion*, a stack-based implementation of recursion. This means that, for every recursive call, there is a new frame in the stack.

To illustrate the problems that can arise from this method, let's use the classic recursive algorithm for factorials.

```
var factorial = function(n) {
  if (n == 0) {
    // base case
    return 1;
  }
  else {
    // recursive case
    return n * factorial(n-1);
  }
}
```

The algorithm will call itself n times to get the answer. It's literally computing (1 x 1 x 2 x 3 x ... x N). That means the time complexity is O(n).

O(n), pronounced "big oh to the n," means that the complexity of the algorithm will grow at a rate of n as the size of the input grows, which is leaner growth. O(n2) is exponential growth, O(log(n)) is logarithmic growth, and so on. This notation can be used for time complexity as well as space complexity.

But, because a new frame in the memory stack is allocated for each iteration, the space complexity is also O(n). This is a problem. This means that memory will be consumed at such a rate the memory limit will be exceeded far too easily. On my laptop, factorial(23456) returns Uncaught Error: RangeError: Maximum call stack size exceeded.

While calculating the factorial of 23,456 is a frivolous endeavor, you can be assured that many problems that are solved with recursion will grow to that size without too much trouble. Consider the case of data trees. The tree could be anything: search applications, file systems, routing tables, and so on. Below is a very simple implementation of the tree traversal function:

```
var traverse = function(node) {
  node.doSomething(); // whatever work needs to be done
  node.childern.forEach(traverse); // many recursive calls
}
```

With just two children per node, both time complexity and space complexity, (in the worst case, where the entire tree must be traversed to find the answer), would be O(n2) because there would be two recursive calls each. With many children per node, the complexity would be O(nm) where m is the number of children. And recursion is the preferred algorithm for tree traversal; a while loop would be much more complex and would require the maintenance of a stack.

Exponential growth like this would mean that it would not take a very large tree to throw a RangeError exception. There must be a better way.

The Tail-call elimination

We need a way to eliminate the allocation of new stack frames for every recursive call. This is known as *tail-call elimination*.

With tail-call elimination, when a function returns the result of calling itself, the language doesn't actually perform another function call. It turns the whole thing into a loop for you.

OK, so how do we do this? With lazy evaluation. If we could rewrite it to fold over a lazy sequence, such that the function returns a value or it returns the result of calling another function without doing anything with that result, then new stack frames don't need to be allocated.

To put it in "tail recursion form", the factorial function would have to be rewritten such that the inner procedure `fact` calls itself last in the control flow, as shown in the following code snippet:

```
var factorial = function(n) {
  var _fact = function(x, n) {
    if (n == 0) {
      // base case
      return x;
    }
    else {
      // recursive case
      return _fact(n*x, n-1);
    }
  }
  return _fact(1, n);
}
```

> Instead of having the result produced by the first function in the recursion tail (like in n * factorial(n-1)), the result is computed going down the recursion tail (with the call to _fact(r*n, n-1)) and is produced by the last function in this tail (with return r;). The computation goes only one way down, not on its way up. It's relatively easy to process it as an iteration for the interpreter.

However, *tail-call elimination does not work in JavaScript*. Put the above code into your favorite JavaScript engine and `factorial(24567)` still returns `Uncaught Error: RangeError: Maximum call stack size exceeded` exception. Tail-call elimination is listed as a new feature to be included in the next release of ECMAScript, but it will be some time before all browsers implement it.

JavaScript cannot optimize functions that are put into tail recursion form. It's a feature of the language specification and runtime interpreter, plain and simple. It has to do with how the interpreter acquires resources for stack frames. Some languages will reuse the same stack frame when it doesn't need to remember anything new, like in the preceding function. This is how tail-call elimination reduces both time and space complexity.

Unfortunately, JavaScript does not do this. But if it did, it would reorganize the stack frames from this:

```
call factorial (3)
  call fact (3 1)
    call fact (2 3)
      call fact (1 6)
        call fact (0 6)
          return 6
        return 6
      return 6
    return 6
  return 6
```

into the following:

```
call factorial (3)
  call fact (3 1)
  call fact (2 3)
  call fact (1 6)
  call fact (0 6)
  return 6
return 6
```

Trampolining

The solution? A process known as **trampolining**. It's a way to "hack" the concept of tail-call elimination into a program by using **thunks**.

> Thunks are, for this purpose, expressions with arguments that wrap anonymous functions with no arguments of their own. For example: `function(str){return function(){console.log(str)}}`. This prevents the expression from being evaluated until a receiving function calls the anonymous function.

A trampoline is a function that takes a function as input and repeatedly executes its returned value until something other than a function is returned. A simple implementation is shown in the following code snippet:

```
var trampoline = function(f) {
  while (f && f instanceof Function) {
    f = f.apply(f.context, f.args);
  }
  return f;
}
```

To actually implement tail-call elimination, we need to use thunks. For this, we can use the `bind()` function that allows us to apply a method to one object with the `this` keyword assigned to another. Internally, it's the same as the `call` keyword, but it's chained to the method and returns a new bound function. The `bind()` function actually does partial application, though in a very limited way.

```
var factorial = function(n) {
  var _fact = function(x, n) {
    if (n == 0) {
      // base case
      return x;
    }
    else {
      // recursive case
      return _fact.bind(null, n*x, n-1);
    }
  }
  return trampoline(_fact.bind(null, 1, n));
}
```

But writing the `fact.bind(null, ...)` method is cumbersome and would confuse anybody reading the code. Instead, let's write our own function for creating thunks. There are a few things the `thunk()` function must do:

- `thunk()` function must emulate the `_fact.bind(null, n*x, n-1)` method that returns a non-evaluated function
- The `thunk()` function should enclose two more functions:
  - For processing the give function, and
  - For processing the function arguments that will be used when the given function is invoked

With that, we're ready to write the function. We only need a few lines of code to write it.

```
var thunk = function (fn) {
  return function() {
    var args = Array.prototype.slice.apply(arguments);
    return function() { return fn.apply(this, args); };
  };
};
```

Now we can use the `thunk()` function in our factorial algorithm like this:

```
var factorial = function(n) {
  var fact = function(x, n) {
    if (n == 0) {
      return x;
    }
    else {
      return thunk(fact)(n * x, n - 1);
    }
  }
  return trampoline(thunk(fact)(1, n));
}
```

But again, we can simplify it just a bit further by defining the `_fact()` function as a `thunk()` function. By defining the inner function as a `thunk()` function, we're relieved of having to use the `thunk()` function both inside the inner function definition and in the return statement.

```
var factorial = function(n) {
  var _fact = thunk(function(x, n) {
    if (n == 0) {
      // base case
      return x;
    }
    else {
      // recursive case
      return _fact(n * x, n - 1);
    }
  });
  return trampoline(_fact(1, n));
}
```

The result is beautiful. What seems like the function `_fact()` being recursively called for a tail-free recursion is almost transparently processed as an iteration!

Finally, let's see how the `trampoline()` and `thunk()` functions work with our more meaningful example of tree traversal. The following is a crude example of how a data tree could be traversed using trampolining and thunks:

```
var treeTraverse = function(trunk) {
  var _traverse = thunk(function(node) {
    node.doSomething();
    node.children.forEach(_traverse);
  }
  trampoline(_traverse(trunk));
}
```

We've solved the issue of tail recursion. But is there an even better way? What if we could simply convert the recursive function to a non-recursive function? Up next, we'll look at how to do just that.

The Y-combinator

The Y-combinator is one of those things in computer science that amaze even the deftest of programming masterminds. Its ability to automatically convert recursive functions to non-recursive functions is why Douglas Crockford calls it "one of the most strange and wonderful artifacts of computer science", and Sussman and Steele once said, "That this manages to work is truly remarkable".

So a truly-remarkable, wonderfully strange artifact of computer science that brings recursive functions to their knees must be massive and complex, right? No, not exactly. Its implementation in JavaScript is only nine, very odd, lines of code. They are as follows:

```
var Y = function(F) {
  return (function (f) {
    return f(f);
  } (function (f) {
    return F(function (x) {
      return f(f)(x);
    });
  }));
}
```

Here's how it works: it finds the "fixed point" of the function passed in as an argument. Fixed points offer another way to think about functions rather than recursion and iteration in the theory of computer programming. And it does this with only the use of anonymous function expressions, function applications, and variable references. Note that Y does not reference itself. In fact, all those functions are anonymous.

As you might have guessed, the Y-combinator came out of lambda calculus. It's actually derived with the help of another combinator called the U-combinator. Combinators are special higher-order functions that only use function application and earlier defined combinators to define a result from its input.

To demonstrate the Y-combinator, we'll again turn to the factorial problem, but we need to define the factorial function a little differently. Instead of writing a recursive function, we write a function that returns a function that is the mathematical definition of factorials. Then we can pass this into the Y-combinator.

```
var FactorialGen = function(factorial) {
  return (function(n) {
    if (n == 0) {
      // base case
      return 1;
    }
    else {
      // recursive case
      return n * factorial(n - 1);
    }
  });
};
Factorial = Y(FactorialGen);
Factorial(10); // 3628800
```

However, when we give it a significantly large number, the stack overflows just as if tail recursion without trampolining was used.

```
Factorial(23456); // RangeError: Maximum call stack size exceeded
```

But we can use trampolining with the Y-combinator as in the following:

```
var FactorialGen2 = function (factorial) {
  return function(n) {
    var factorial = thunk(function (x, n) {
      if (n == 0) {
        return x;
      }
      else {
        return factorial(n * x, n - 1);
      }
    });
    return trampoline(factorial(1, n));
  }
};

var Factorial2 = Y(FactorialGen2)
Factorial2(10); // 3628800
Factorial2(23456); // Infinity
```

We can also rearrange the Y-combinator to perform something called memoization.

Memoization

Memoization is the technique of storing the result of expensive function calls. When the function is later called with the same arguments, the stored result is returned rather than computing the result again.

Although the Y-combinator is much faster than recursion, it is still relatively slow. To speed it up, we can create a memoizing fixed-point combinator: a Y-like combinator that caches the results of intermediate function calls.

```javascript
var Ymem = function(F, cache) {
  if (!cache) {
    cache = {} ; // Create a new cache.
  }
  return function(arg) {
    if (cache[arg]) {
      // Answer in cache
      return cache[arg] ;
    }
    // else compute the answer
    var answer = (F(function(n){
      return (Ymem(F,cache))(n);
    }))(arg); // Compute the answer.
    cache[arg] = answer; // Cache the answer.
    return answer;
  };
}
```

So how much faster is it? By using `http://jsperf.com/`, we can compare the performance.

The following results are with random numbers between 1 and 100. We can see that the memoizing Y-combinator is much, much faster. And adding trampolining to it does not slow it down by much. You can view the results and run the tests yourself at this URL: `http://jsperf.com/memoizing-y-combinator-vs-tail-call-optimization/7`.

Chapter 6

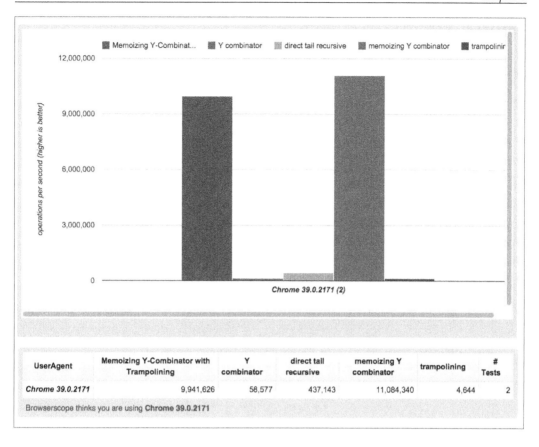

The bottom line is: the most efficient and safest method of performing recursion in JavaScript is to use the memoizing Y-combinator with tail-call elimination via trampolining and thunks.

Variable scope

The scope of variables in JavaScript is not natural. In fact, sometimes it's downright counter-intuitive. They say that JavaScript programmers can be judged by how well they understand scope.

Scope resolutions

First, let's go over the different scope resolutions in JavaScript.

JavaScript uses scope chains to establish the scope of variables. When resolving a variable, it starts at the innermost scope and searches outwards.

Global scope

Variables, functions, and objects defined at this level are available to any code in the entire program. This is the outermost scope.

```
var x = 'hi';
function a() {
   console.log(x);
}
a(); // 'hi'
```

Local scope

Each function described has its own local scope. Any function defined within another function has a nested local scope that is linked to the outer function. Almost always, it's the position in the source that defines the scope.

```
var x = 'hi';
function a() {
   console.log(x);
}
function b() {
   var x = 'hello';
   console.log(x);
}
b(); // hello
a(); // hi
```

Local scope is only for functions and not for any expression statements (`if`, `for`, `while`, and so on), which is different from how most languages treat scope.

```
function c() {
   var y = 'greetings';
   if (true) {
      var y = 'guten tag';
   }
   console.log(y);
}

function d() {
   var y = 'greetings';
   function e() {
      var y = 'guten tag';
   }
```

```
    console.log(y)
}
c(); // 'guten tag'
d(); // 'greetings'
```

In functional programming, this isn't as much of a concern because functions are used more often and expression statements less often. For example:

```
function e(){
  var z = 'namaste';
  [1,2,3].foreach(function(n) {
    var z = 'aloha';
  }
  isTrue(function(){
    var z = 'good morning';
  });
  console.log(z);
}
e(); // 'namaste'
```

Object properties

Object properties have their own scope chains as well.

```
var x = 'hi';
var obj = function(){
  this.x = 'hola';
};
var foo = new obj();
console.log(foo.x); // 'hola'
foo.x = 'bonjour';
console.log(foo.x); // 'bonjour'
```

The object's prototype is further down the scope chain.

```
obj.prototype.x = 'greetings';
obj.prototype.y = 'konnichi ha';
var bar = new obj();
console.log(bar.x); // still prints 'hola'
console.log(bar.y); // 'konnichi ha'
```

This isn't even close to being comprehensive, but these three types of scope are enough to get started.

Closures

One problem with this scope structure is that it leaves no room for private variables. Consider the following code snippet:

```
var name = 'Ford Focus';
var year = '2006';
var millage = 123456;
function getMillage(){
  return millage;
}
function updateMillage(n) {
  millage = n;
}
```

These variables and functions are global, which means it would be too easy for code later down the program to accidentally overwrite them. One solution would be to encapsulate them into a function and call that function immediately after defining it.

```
var car = function(){
  var name = 'Ford Focus';
  var year = '2006';
  var millage = 123456;
  function getMillage(){
    return Millage;
  }
  function updateMillage(n) {
    millage = n;
  }
}();
```

Nothing is happening outside the function, so we ought to discard the function name by making it anonymous.

```
(function(){
  var name = 'Ford Focus';
  var year = '2006';
  var millage = 123456;
  function getMillage(){
    return millage;
  }
  function updateMillage(n) {
    millage = n;
  }
})();
```

To make the functions `getValue()` and `updateMillage()` available outside the anonymous function, we'll need to return them in an object literal as shown in the following code snippet:

```
var car = function(){
  var name = 'Ford Focus';
  var year = '2006';
  var millage = 123456;
  return {
    getMillage: function(){
      return millage;
    },
    updateMillage: function(n) {
      millage = n;
    }
  }
}();
console.log( car.getMillage() ); // works
console.log( car.updateMillage(n) ); // also works
console.log( car.millage ); // undefined
```

This gives us pseudo-private variables, but the problems don't stop there. The following section explores more issues with variable scope in JavaScript.

Gotchas

Many variable scope nuances can be found throughout JavaScript. The following is by no means a comprehensive list, but it covers the most common cases:

- The following will output 4, not 'undefined' as one would expect:

    ```
    for (var n = 4; false; ) { } console.log(n);
    ```

    This is due to the fact that, in JavaScript, variable definition happens at the beginning of the corresponding scope, not just when it is declared.

- If you define a variable in the outer scope, and then have an `if` statement define a variable inside the function with the same name, even if that `if` branch isn't reached, it is redefined. An example:

    ```
    var x = 1;
    function foo() {
      if (false) {
        var x = 2;
      }
      return x;
    ```

```
}
foo(); // Return value: 'undefined', expected return value:
2
```

Again, this is caused by moving the variable definition at the beginning of the scope with the `undefined` value.

- In the browser, global variables are really stored in the `window` object.

    ```
    window.a = 19;
    console.log(a); // Output: 19
    ```

    `a` in the global scope means `a` as an attribute of the current context, so `a===this.a` and `window` object in a browser act as an equivalent of the `this` keyword in the global scope.

The first two examples are a result of a feature of JavaScript known as hoisting, which will be a critical concept in the next section about writing functions.

Function declarations versus function expressions versus the function constructor

What is the difference between these three statements?

```
function foo(n){ return n; }
var foo = function(n){ return n; };
var foo = new Function('n', 'return n');
```

At first glance, they're merely different ways to write the same function. But there's a little more going on here. And if we're to take full advantage of functions in JavaScript in order to manipulate them into a functional programming style, then we'd better be able to get this right. If there is a better way to do something in computer programming, then that one way should be the only way.

Function declarations

Function declarations, sometimes called function statements, define a function by using the `function` keyword.

```
function foo(n) {
  return n;
}
```

Functions that are declared with this syntax are *hoisted* to the top of the current scope. What this actually means is that, even if the function is defined several lines down, JavaScript knows about it and can use it earlier in the scope. For example, the following will correctly print 6 to the console:

```
foo(2,3);
function foo(n, m) {
   console.log(n*m);
}
```

Function expressions

Named functions can also be defined as an expression by defining an anonymous function and assigning it to a variable.

```
var bar = function(n, m) {
   console.log(n*m);
};
```

They are not hoisted like function declarations are. This is because, while function declarations are hoisted, variable declarations are not. For example, this will not work and will throw an error:

```
bar(2,3);
var bar = function(n, m) {
   console.log(n*m);
};
```

In functional programming, we're going to want to use function expressions so we can treat the functions like variables, making them available to be used as callbacks and arguments to higher-order functions such as `map()` functions. Defining functions as expressions makes it more obvious that they're variables assigned to a function. Also, if we're going to write functions in one style, we should write all functions in that style for the sake of consistency and clarity.

The function constructor

JavaScript actually has a third way to create functions: with the `Function()` constructor. Just like function expressions, functions defined with the `Function()` constructor are not hoisted.

```
var func = new Function('n','m','return n+m');
func(2,3); // returns 5
```

But the `Function()` constructor is not only confusing, it is also highly dangerous. No syntax correction can happen, no optimization is possible. It's far easier, safer, and less confusing to write the same function as follows:

```
var func = function(n,m){return n+m};
func(2,3); // returns 5
```

Unpredictable behavior

So the difference is that function declarations are hoisted while function expressions are not. This can cause unexpected things to happen. Consider the following:

```
function foo() {
   return 'hi';
}
console.log(foo());
function foo() {
   return 'hello';
}
```

What's actually printed to the console is `hello`. This is due to the fact that the second definition of the `foo()` function is hoisted to the top, making it the definition that is actually used by the JavaScript interpreter.

While at first this may not seem like a critical difference, in functional programming this can cause mayhem. Consider the following code snippet:

```
if (true) {
   function foo(){console.log('one')};
}
else {
   function foo(){console.log('two')};
}
foo();
```

When the `foo()` function is called, `two` is printed to the console, not `one`!

Finally, there is a way to combine both function expressions and declarations. It works as follows:

```
var foo = function bar(){ console.log('hi'); };
foo(); // 'hi'
bar(); // Error: bar is not defined
```

It makes very little sense to use this method because the name used in the declaration (the `bar()` function in the preceding example) is not available outside the function and causes confusion. It would only be appropriate for recursion, for example:

```
var foo = function factorial(n) {
  if (n == 0) {
     return 1;
  }
  else {
     return n * factorial(n-1);
  }
};
foo(5);
```

Summary

JavaScript has been called the "assembly language of the web," because it's as ubiquitous and unavoidable as x86 assembly. It's the only language that runs on all browsers. It's also flawed, yet referring to it as a low-level language is missing the mark.

Instead, think of JavaScript as the raw coffee beans of the web. Sure, some of the beans are damaged and a few are rotten. But if the good ones are selected, roasted, and brewed by a skilled barista, the beans can be transformed into a brilliant jamocha that cannot be had just once and forgotten. It's consumption becomes a daily custom, life without it would be static, harder to perform, and much less exciting. Some even prefer to enhance the brew with plug-ins and add-ons such as cream, sugar, and cocoa, which complement it very well.

One of JavaScript's biggest critics, Douglas Crawford, was quoted as saying "There are certainly a lot of people who refuse to consider the possibility that JavaScript got anything right. I used to be one of those guys. But now I continue to be amazed by the brilliance that is in there".

JavaScript turned out to be pretty awesome.

7
Functional and Object-oriented Programming in JavaScript

You will often hear that JavaScript is a blank language, where blank is either object-oriented, functional, or general-purpose. This book has focused on JavaScript as a functional language and has gone to great lengths to prove that it is. But the truth is that JavaScript is a general-purpose language, meaning it's fully capable of multiple programming styles. Like Python and F#, JavaScript is multi-paradigm. But unlike those languages, JavaScript's OOP side is prototype-based while most other general-purpose languages are class-based.

In this final chapter, we will relate both functional and object-oriented programming to JavaScript, and see how the two paradigms can complement each other and coexist side-by-side. In this chapter the following topics will be covered:

- How can JavaScript be both functional and OOP?
- JavaScript's OOP – using prototypes
- How to mix functional and OOP in JavaScript
- Functional inheritance
- Functional mixins

Better code is the goal. Functional and object-oriented programming are just means to this end.

JavaScript – the multi-paradigm language

If object-oriented programming means treating all variables as objects, and functional programming means treating all functions as variables, then can't functions be treated like objects? In JavaScript, they can.

But saying that functional programming means treating functions as variables is somewhat inaccurate. A better way to put it is: functional programming means treating everything as a value, especially functions.

A better way still to describe functional programming may be to call it declarative. Independent of the imperative branch of programming styles, *declarative programming* expresses the logic of computation required to solve the problem. The computer is told what the problem is rather than the procedure for how to solve it.

Meanwhile, object-oriented programming is derived from the imperative programming style: the computer is given step-by-step instructions for how to solve the problem. OOP mandates that the instructions for computation (methods) and the data they work on (member variables) be organized into units called objects. The only way to access that data is through the object's methods.

So how can these two styles be integrated together?

- The code inside the object's methods is typically written in an imperative style. But what if it was in a functional style? After all, OOP doesn't exclude immutable data and higher-order functions.
- Perhaps a purer way to mix the two would be to treat objects both as functions and as traditional, class-based objects at the same time.
- Maybe we can simply include several ideas from functional programming — such as promises and recursion — into our object-oriented application.
- OOP covers topics such as encapsulation, polymorphism, and abstraction. So does functional programming, it just goes about it in a different way. So maybe we can include several ideas from object-oriented programming in our functional-oriented application.

The point is: OOP and FP can be mixed together and there are several ways to do it. They're not exclusive of each other.

JavaScript's object-oriented implementation – using prototypes

JavaScript is a class-less language. That's not to mean it is less fashionable or more blue-collar than other computer languages; class-less means it doesn't have a class structure in the same way that object-oriented languages do. Instead, it uses prototypes for inheritance.

Although this may be baffling to programmers with backgrounds in C++ and Java, prototype-based inheritance can be much more expressive than traditional inheritance. The following is a brief comparison between the differences between C++ and JavaScript:

C++	JavaScript
Strongly typed	Loosely typed
Static	Dynamic
Class-based	Prototype-based
Classes	Functions
Constructors	Functions
Methods	Functions

Inheritance

Before we go much further, let's make sure we fully understand the concept of inheritance in object-oriented programming. Class-based inheritance is demonstrated in the following pseudo-code:

```
class Polygon {
  int numSides;
  function init(n) {
    numSides = n;
  }
}
class Rectangle inherits Polygon {
  int width;
  int length;
  function init(w, l) {
    numSides = 4;
    width = w;
    length = l;
  }
```

```
    function getArea() {
      return w * l;
    }
  }
  class Square inherits Rectangle {
    function init(s) {
      numSides = 4;
      width = s;
      length = s;
    }
  }
```

The `Polygon` class is the parent class the other classes inherit from. It defines just one member variable, the number of sides, which is set in the `init()` function. The `Rectangle` subclass inherits from the `Polygon` class and adds two more member variables, `length` and `width`, and a method, `getArea()`. It doesn't need to define the `numSides` variable because it was already defined by the class it inherits from, and it also overrides the `init()` function. The `Square` class carries on this chain of inheritance even further by inheriting from the `Rectangle` class for its `getArea()` method. By simply overriding the `init()` function again such that the length and width are the same, the `getArea()` function can remain unchanged and less code needs to be written.

In a traditional OOP language, this is what inheritance is all about. If we wanted to add a color property to all the objects, all we would have to do is add it to the `Polygon` object without having to modify any of the objects that inherit from it.

JavaScript's prototype chain

Inheritance in JavaScript comes down to prototypes. Each object has an internal property known as its prototype, which is a link to another object. That object has a prototype of its own. This pattern can repeat until an object is reached that has `undefined` as its prototype. This is known as the prototype chain, and it's how inheritance works in JavaScript. The following diagram explain the inheritance in JavaScirpt:

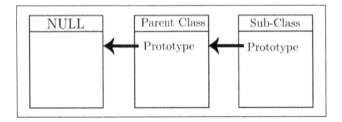

When running a search for an object's function definition, JavaScript "walks" the prototype chain until it finds the first definition of a function with the right name. Therefore, overriding it is as simple as providing a new definition on the prototype of the subclass.

Inheritance in JavaScript and the Object.create() method

Just as there are many ways to create objects in JavaScript, there are also many ways to replicate class-based, classical inheritance. But the one preferred way to do it is with the `Object.create()` method.

```
var Polygon = function(n) {
  this.numSides = n;
}

var Rectangle = function(w, l) {
  this.width = w;
  this.length = l;
}

// the Rectangle's prototype is redefined with Object.create
Rectangle.prototype = Object.create(Polygon.prototype);

// it's important to now restore the constructor attribute
// otherwise it stays linked to the Polygon
Rectangle.prototype.constructor = Rectangle;

// now we can continue to define the Rectangle class
Rectangle.prototype.numSides = 4;
Rectangle.prototype.getArea = function() {
  return this.width * this.length;
}

var Square = function(w) {
  this.width = w;
  this.length = w;
}
Square.prototype = Object.create(Rectangle.prototype);
Square.prototype.constructor = Square;

var s = new Square(5);
console.log( s.getArea() ); // 25
```

This syntax may seem unusual to many but, with a little practice, it will become familiar. The `prototype` keyword must be used to gain access to the internal property, `[[Prototype]]`, which all objects have. The `Object.create()` method declares a new object with a specified object for its prototype to inherit from. In this way, classical inheritance can be achieved in JavaScript.

 The `Object.create()` method was introduced in ECMAScript 5.1 in 2011, and it was billed as the new and preferred way to create objects. This was just one of many attempts to integrate inheritance into JavaScript. Thankfully, this method works pretty well.

We saw this structure of inheritance when building the `Maybe` classes in *Chapter 5, Category Theory*. Here are the `Maybe`, `None`, and `Just` classes, which inherit from each other just like the preceding example.

```
var Maybe = function(){};

var None = function(){};
None.prototype = Object.create(Maybe.prototype);
None.prototype.constructor = None;
None.prototype.toString = function(){return 'None';};

var Just = function(x){this.x = x;};
Just.prototype = Object.create(Maybe.prototype);
Just.prototype.constructor = Just;
Just.prototype.toString = function(){return "Just "+this.x;};
```

This shows that class inheritance in JavaScript can be an enabler of functional programming.

A common mistake is to pass a constructor into `Object.create()` instead of a `prototype` object. This problem is compounded by the fact that an error will not be thrown until the subclass tries to use an inherited member function.

```
Foo.prototype = Object.create(Parent.prototype); // correct
Bar.prototype = Object.create(Parent); // incorrect
Bar.inheritedMethod(); // Error: function is undefined
```

The function won't be found if the `inheritedMethod()` method has been attached to the `Foo.prototype` class. If the `inheritedMethod()` method is attached directly to the instance with `this.inheritedMethod = function(){...}` in the `Bar` constructor, then this use of `Parent` as an argument of `Object.create()` could be correct.

Mixing functional and object-oriented programming in JavaScript

Object-oriented programming has been the dominant programming paradigm for several decades. It is taught in Computer Science 101 classes around the world, while functional programming is not. It is what software architects use to design applications, while functional programming is not. And it makes sense too: OOP makes it easy to conceptualize abstract ideas. It makes it easier to write code.

So, unless you can convince your boss that the application needs to be all functional, we're going to be using functional programming in an object-oriented world. This section will explore ways to do this.

Functional inheritance

Perhaps the most accessible way to apply functional programming to JavaScript applications is to use a mostly functional style within OOP principles, such as inheritance.

To explore how this might work, let's build a simple application that calculates the price of a product. First, we'll need some product classes:

```
var Shirt = function(size) {
  this.size = size;
};

var TShirt = function(size) {
  this.size = size;
};
TShirt.prototype = Object.create(Shirt.prototype);
TShirt.prototype.constructor = TShirt;
TShirt.prototype.getPrice = function(){
  if (this.size == 'small') {
    return 5;
  }
  else {
    return 10;
  }
}

var ExpensiveShirt = function(size) {
  this.size = size;
}
```

```
ExpensiveShirt.prototype = Object.create(Shirt.prototype);
ExpensiveShirt.prototype.constructor = ExpensiveShirt;
ExpensiveShirt.prototype.getPrice = function() {
  if (this.size == 'small') {
    return 20;
  }
  else {
    return 30;
  }
}
```

We can then organize them within a `Store` class as follows:

```
var Store = function(products) {
  this.products = products;
}
Store.prototype.calculateTotal = function(){
  return this.products.reduce(function(sum,product) {
    return sum + product.getPrice();
  }, 10) * TAX; // start with $10 markup, times global TAX var
};

var TAX = 1.08;
var p1 = new TShirt('small');
var p2 = new ExpensiveShirt('large');
var s = new Store([p1,p2]);
console.log(s.calculateTotal()); // Output: 35
```

The `calculateTotal()` method uses the array's `reduce()` function to cleanly sum together the prices of the products.

This works just fine, but what if we need a dynamic way to calculate the markup value? For this, we can turn to a concept called **Strategy Pattern**.

Strategy Pattern

Strategy Pattern is a method for defining a family of interchangeable algorithms. It is used by OOP programmers to manipulate behavior at runtime, but it is based on a few functional programming principles:

- Separation of logic and data
- Composition of functions
- Functions as first-class objects

And a couple of OOP principles as well:

- Encapsulation
- Inheritance

In our example application for calculating product cost, explained previously, let's say we want to give preferential treatment to certain customers, and that the markup will have to be adjusted to reflect this.

So let's create some customer classes:

```
var Customer = function(){};
Customer.prototype.calculateTotal = function(products) {
  return products.reduce(function(total, product) {
    return total + product.getPrice();
  }, 10) * TAX;
};

var RepeatCustomer = function(){};
RepeatCustomer.prototype = Object.create(Customer.prototype);
RepeatCustomer.prototype.constructor = RepeatCustomer;
RepeatCustomer.prototype.calculateTotal = function(products) {
  return products.reduce(function(total, product) {
    return total + product.getPrice();
  }, 5) * TAX;
};

var TaxExemptCustomer = function(){};
TaxExemptCustomer.prototype = Object.create(Customer.prototype);
TaxExemptCustomer.prototype.constructor = TaxExemptCustomer;
TaxExemptCustomer.prototype.calculateTotal = function(products) {
  return products.reduce(function(total, product) {
    return total + product.getPrice();
  }, 10);
};
```

Each `Customer` class encapsulates the algorithm. Now we just need the `Store` class to call the `Customer` class's `calculateTotal()` method.

```
var Store = function(products) {
  this.products = products;
  this.customer = new Customer();
  // bonus exercise: use Maybes from Chapter 5 instead of a
  default customer instance
}
```

```
Store.prototype.setCustomer = function(customer) {
  this.customer = customer;
}
Store.prototype.getTotal = function(){
  return this.customer.calculateTotal(this.products);
};

var p1 = new TShirt('small');
var p2 = new ExpensiveShirt('large');
var s = new Store([p1,p2]);
var c = new TaxExemptCustomer();
s.setCustomer(c);
s.getTotal(); // Output: 45
```

The `Customer` classes do the calculating, the `Product` classes hold the data (the prices), and the `Store` class maintains the context. This achieves a very high level of cohesion and a very good mixture of object-oriented programming and functional programming. JavaScript's high level of expressiveness makes this possible and quite easy.

Mixins

In a nutshell, mixins are classes that can allow other classes to use their methods. The methods are intended to be used solely by other classes, and the `mixin` class itself is never to be instantiated. This helps to avoid inheritance ambiguity. And they're a great means of mixing functional programming with object-oriented programming.

Mixins are implemented differently in each language. Thanks to JavaScript's flexibility and expressiveness, mixins are implemented as objects with only methods. While they can be defined as function objects (that is, `var mixin = function(){...};`), it would be better for the structural discipline of the code to define them as object literals (that is, `var mixin = {...};`). This will help us to distinguish between classes and mixins. After all, mixins should be treated as processes, not objects.

Let's start with declaring some mixins. We'll extend our `Store` application from the previous section, using mixins to expand on the classes.

```
var small = {
  getPrice: function() {
    return this.basePrice + 6;
  },
  getDimensions: function() {
    return [44,63]
  }
```

```
}
var large = {
  getPrice: function() {
    return this.basePrice + 10;
  },
  getDimensions: function() {
    return [64,83]
  }
};
```

We're not limited to just this. Many more mixins can be added, like colors or fabric material. We'll have to rewrite our Shirt classes a little bit, as shown in the following code snippet:

```
var Shirt = function() {
  this.basePrice = 1;
};
Shirt.getPrice = function(){
  return this.basePrice;
}
var TShirt = function() {
  this.basePrice = 5;
};
TShirt.prototype = Object.create(Shirt.prototype);
TShirt..prototype.constructor = TShirt;
```

Now we're ready to use mixins.

Classical mixins

You're probably wondering just how these mixins get mixed with the classes. The classical way to do this is by copying the mixin's functions into the receiving object. This can be done with the following extension to the Shirt prototype:

```
Shirt.prototype.addMixin = function (mixin) {
  for (var prop in mixin) {
    if (mixin.hasOwnProperty(prop)) {
      this.prototype[prop] = mixin[prop];
    }
  }
};
```

And now the mixins can be added as follows:

```
TShirt.addMixin(small);
var p1 = new TShirt();
console.log( p1.getPrice() ); // Output: 11

TShirt.addMixin(large);
var p2 = new TShirt();
console.log( p2.getPrice() ); // Output: 15
```

However, there is a major problem. When the price of p1 is calculated again, it comes back as 15, the price of a large item. It should be the value for a small one!

```
console.log( p1.getPrice() ); // Output: 15
```

The problem is that the Shirt object's prototype.getPrice() method is getting rewritten every time a mixin is added to it; this is not very functional at all and not what we want.

Functional mixins

There's another way to use mixins, one that is more aligned with functional programming.

Instead of copying the methods of the mixin to the target object, we need to create a new object that is a clone of the target object with the mixin's methods added in. The object must be cloned first, and this is achieved by creating a new object that inherits from it. We'll call this variation plusMixin.

```
Shirt.prototype.plusMixin = function(mixin) {
  // create a new object that inherits from the old
  var newObj = this;
  newObj.prototype = Object.create(this.prototype);
  for (var prop in mixin) {
    if (mixin.hasOwnProperty(prop)) {
      newObj.prototype[prop] = mixin[prop];
    }
  }
  return newObj;
};

var SmallTShirt = Tshirt.plusMixin(small); // creates a new class
var smallT = new SmallTShirt();
console.log( smallT.getPrice() );   // Output: 11
```

```
var LargeTShirt = Tshirt.plusMixin(large);
var largeT = new LargeTShirt();
console.log( largeT.getPrice() ); // Output: 15
console.log( smallT.getPrice() ); // Output: 11 (not effected by 2nd
mixin call)
```

Here comes the fun part! Now we can get really functional with the mixins. We can create every possible combination of products and mixins.

```
// in the real world there would be way more products and mixins!
var productClasses = [ExpensiveShirt, Tshirt];
var mixins = [small, medium, large];

// mix them all together
products = productClasses.reduce(function(previous, current) {
  var newProduct = mixins.map(function(mxn) {
    var mixedClass = current.plusMixin(mxn);
    var temp = new mixedClass();
    return temp;
  });
  return previous.concat(newProduct);
},[]);
products.forEach(function(o){console.log(o.getPrice())});
```

To make it more object-oriented, we can rewrite the Store object with this functionality. We'll also add a display function to the Store object, not the products, to keep the interface logic and the data separated.

```
// the store
var Store = function() {
  productClasses = [ExpensiveShirt, TShirt];
  productMixins = [small, medium, large];
  this.products = productClasses.reduce(function(previous,
  current) {
    var newObjs = productMixins.map(function(mxn) {
      var mixedClass = current.plusMixin(mxn);
      var temp = new mixedClass();
      return temp;
    });
    return previous.concat(newObjs);
  },[]);
}
Store.prototype.displayProducts = function(){
  this.products.forEach(function(p) {
    $('ul#products').append('<li>'+p.getTitle()+':
    $'+p.getPrice()+'</li>');
  });
}
```

And all we have to do is create a `Store` object and call its `displayProducts()` method to generate a list of products and prices!

```
<ul id="products">
  <li>small premium shirt: $16</li>
  <li>medium premium shirt: $18</li>
  <li>large premium shirt: $20</li>
  <li>small t-shirt: $11</li>
  <li>medium t-shirt: $13</li>
  <li>large t-shirt: $15</li>
</ul>
```

These lines need to be added to the `product` classes and mixins to get the preceding output to work:

```
Shirt.prototype.title = 'shirt';
TShirt.prototype.title = 't-shirt';
ExpensiveShirt.prototype.title = 'premium shirt';

// then the mixins got the extra 'getTitle' function:
var small = {
  ...
  getTitle: function() {
    return 'small ' + this.title; // small or medium or large
  }
}
```

And, just like that, we have an e-commerce application that is highly modular and extendable. New shirt styles can be added absurdly easily — just define a new `Shirt` subclass and add to it the `Store` class's array `product` classes. Mixins are added in just the same way. So now when our boss says, "Hey, we have a new type of shirt and a coat, each available in the standard colors, and we need them added to the website before you go home today", we can rest assured that we'll not be staying late!

Summary

JavaScript has a high level of expressiveness. This makes it possible to mix functional and object-oriented programming. Modern JavaScript is not solely OOP or functional—it is a mixture of the two. Concepts such as Strategy Pattern and mixins are perfect for JavaScript's prototype structure, and they help to prove that today's best practices in JavaScript share equal amounts of functional programming and object-oriented programming.

If you were to take away only one thing from this book, I would want it to be how to apply functional programming techniques to real-world applications. And this chapter showed you how to do exactly that.

A
Common Functions for Functional Programming in JavaScript

This Appendix covers common functions for functional programming in JavaScript:

- Array Functions:

    ```
    var flatten = function(arrays) {
      return arrays.reduce( function(p,n){
        return p.concat(n);
      });
    };

    var invert = function(arr) {
      return arr.map(function(x, i, a) {
        return a[a.length - (i+1)];
      });
    };
    ```

- Binding Functions:

    ```
    var bind = Function.prototype.call.bind(Function.prototype.bind);
    var call = bind(Function.prototype.call, Function.prototype.call);
    var apply = bind(Function.prototype.call,
    Function.prototype.apply);
    ```

- Category Theory:

    ```
    var checkTypes = function( typeSafeties ) {
      arrayOf(func)(arr(typeSafeties));
    ```

```
      var argLength = typeSafeties.length;
      return function(args) {
        arr(args);
        if (args.length != argLength) {
          throw new TypeError('Expected '+ argLength + '
          arguments');
        }
        var results = [];
        for (var i=0; i<argLength; i++) {
          results[i] = typeSafeties[i](args[i]);
        }
        return results;
      };
    };

    var homoMorph = function( /* arg1, arg2, ..., argN, output */ ) {
      var before =
      checkTypes(arrayOf(func)(Array.prototype.slice.call
      (arguments, 0, arguments.length-1)));
      var after = func(arguments[arguments.length-1])
      return function(middle) {
        return function(args) {
          return after(middle.apply(this,
          before([].slice.apply(arguments))));
        };
      };
    };
```

- Composition:

```
    Function.prototype.compose = function(prevFunc) {
      var nextFunc = this;
      return function() {
        return
        nextFunc.call(this,prevFunc.apply(this,arguments));
      };
    };

    Function.prototype.sequence  = function(prevFunc) {
      var nextFunc = this;
      return function() {
        return
        prevFunc.call(this,nextFunc.apply(this,arguments));
      };
    };
```

Appendix A

- Currying:
  ```
  Function.prototype.curry = function (numArgs) {
    var func = this;
    numArgs = numArgs || func.length;
    // recursively acquire the arguments
    function subCurry(prev) {
      return function (arg) {
        var args = prev.concat(arg);
        if (args.length < numArgs) {
          // recursive case: we still need more args
          return subCurry(args);
        }
        else {
          // base case: apply the function
          return func.apply(this, args);
        }
      };
    };
    return subCurry([]);
  };
  ```

- Functors:
  ```
  // map :: (a -> b) -> [a] -> [b]
  var map = function(f, a) {
    return arr(a).map(func(f));
  }

  // strmap :: (str -> str) -> str -> str
  var strmap = function(f, s) {
    return str(s).split('').map(func(f)).join('');
  }

  // fcompose :: (a -> b)* -> (a -> b)
  var fcompose = function() {
    var funcs = arrayOf(func)(arguments);
    return function() {
      var argsOfFuncs = arguments;
      for (var i = funcs.length; i > 0; i -= 1) {
        argsOfFuncs = [funcs[i].apply(this, args)];
      }
      return args[0];
    };
  };
  ```

- Lenses:
  ```
  var lens = function(get, set) {
    var f = function (a) {return get(a)};
    f.get = function (a) {return get(a)};
    f.set = set;
    f.mod = function (f, a) {return set(a, f(get(a)))};
    return f;
  };

  // usage:
  var first = lens(
    function (a) { return arr(a)[0]; }, // get
    function (a, b) { return [b].concat(arr(a).slice(1)); } // set
  );
  ```
- Maybes:
  ```
  var Maybe = function(){};
  Maybe.prototype.orElse = function(y) {
    if (this instanceof Just) {
      return this.x;
    }
    else {
      return y;
    }
  };

  var None = function(){};
  None.prototype = Object.create(Maybe.prototype);
  None.prototype.toString = function(){return 'None';};
  var none = function(){return new None()};
  // and the Just instance, a wrapper for an object with a value
  var Just = function(x){return this.x = x;};
  Just.prototype = Object.create(Maybe.prototype);
  Just.prototype.toString = function(){return "Just "+this.x;};
  var just = function(x) {return new Just(x)};
  var maybe = function(m){
    if (m instanceof None) {
      return m;
    }
    else if (m instanceof Just) {
      return just(m.x);
    }
  ```

```
      else {
        throw new TypeError("Error: Just or None expected, " +
        m.toString() + " given.");
      }
    };

    var maybeOf = function(f){
      return function(m) {
        if (m instanceof None) {
          return m;
        }
        else if (m instanceof Just) {
          return just(f(m.x));
        }
        else {
          throw new TypeError("Error: Just or None expected, "
          + m.toString() + " given.");
        }
      };
    };
```

- Mixins:
  ```
  Object.prototype.plusMixin = function(mixin) {
    var newObj = this;
    newObj.prototype = Object.create(this.prototype);
    newObj.prototype.constructor = newObj;
    for (var prop in mixin) {
      if (mixin.hasOwnProperty(prop)) {
        newObj.prototype[prop] = mixin[prop];
      }
    }
    return newObj;
  };
  ```

- Partial Application:
  ```
  function bindFirstArg(func, a) {
    return function(b) {
      return func(a, b);
    };
  };

  Function.prototype.partialApply = function(){
    var func = this;
    args = Array.prototype.slice.call(arguments);
  ```

```
      return function(){
        return func.apply(this, args.concat(
          Array.prototype.slice.call(arguments)
        ));
      };
    };

    Function.prototype.partialApplyRight = function(){
      var func = this;
      args = Array.prototype.slice.call(arguments);
      return function(){
        return func.apply(
          this,
          Array.protype.slice.call(arguments, 0)
          .concat(args));
      };
    };
```

- Trampolining:

```
    var trampoline = function(f) {
      while (f && f instanceof Function) {
        f = f.apply(f.context, f.args);
      }
      return f;
    };

    var thunk = function (fn) {
      return function() {
        var args = Array.prototype.slice.apply(arguments);
        return function() { return fn.apply(this, args); };
      };
    };
```

- Type Safeties:

```
    var typeOf = function(type) {
      return function(x) {
        if (typeof x === type) {
          return x;
        }
        else {
          throw new TypeError("Error: "+type+" expected, "+typeof x+" given.");
        }
      };
```

```
    };

    var str = typeOf('string'),
      num = typeOf('number'),
      func = typeOf('function'),
      bool = typeOf('boolean');

    var objectTypeOf = function(name) {
      return function(o) {
        if (Object.prototype.toString.call(o) === "[object
        "+name+"]") {
          return o;
        }
        else {
          throw new TypeError("Error: '+name+' expected,
          something else given.");
        }
      };
    };
    var obj = objectTypeOf('Object');
    var arr = objectTypeOf('Array');
    var date = objectTypeOf('Date');
    var div = objectTypeOf('HTMLDivElement');

    // arrayOf :: (a -> b) -> ([a] -> [b])
    var arrayOf = function(f) {
      return function(a) {
        return map(func(f), arr(a));
      }
    };
```

- Y-combinator:

```
    var Y = function(F) {
      return (function (f) {
        return f(f);
      }(function (f) {
        return F(function (x) {
          return f(f)(x);
        });
      }));
    };

    // Memoizing Y-Combinator:
    var Ymem = function(F, cache) {
```

```
      if (!cache) {
        cache = {} ; // Create a new cache.
      }
      return function(arg) {
        if (cache[arg]) {
          // Answer in cache
          return cache[arg] ;
        }
        // else compute the answer
        var answer = (F(function(n){
          return (Ymem(F,cache))(n);
        }))(arg); // Compute the answer.
        cache[arg] = answer; // Cache the answer.
        return answer;
      };
    };
```

B
Glossary of Terms

This appendix covers some of the important terms that are used in this book:

- **Anonymous function**: A function that has no name and is not bound to any variables. It is also known as a Lambda Expression.
- **Callback**: A function that can be passed to another function to be used in a later event.
- **Category**: In terms of Category Theory, a category is a collection of objects of the same type. In JavaScript, a category can be an array or object that contains objects that are all explicitly declared as numbers, strings, Booleans, dates, objects, and so on.
- **Category Theory**: A concept that organizes mathematical structures into collections of objects and operations on those objects. The data types and functions used in computer programs form the categories used in this book.
- **Closure**: An environment such that functions defined within it can access local variables that are not available outside it.
- **Coupling**: The degree to which each program module relies on each of the other modules. Functional programming reduces the amount of coupling within a program.
- **Currying**: The process of transforming a function with many arguments into a function with one argument that returns another function that can take more arguments, as needed. Formally, a function with N arguments can be transformed into a function chain of N functions, each with only one argument.
- **Declarative programming**: A programming style that expresses the computational logic required to solve the problem. The computer is told what the problem is rather than the procedure required to solve it.

- **Endofunctor**: A functor that maps a category to itself.
- **Function composition**: The process of combining many functions into one function. The result of each function is passed as an argument to the next, and the result of the last function is the result of the whole composition.
- **Functional language**: A computer language that facilitates functional programming.
- **Functional programming**: A declarative programming paradigm that focuses on treating functions as mathematical expressions and avoids mutable data and changes in state.
- **Functional reactive programming**: A style of functional programming that focuses on reactive elements and variables that change over time in response to events.
- **Functor**: A mapping between categories.
- **Higher-order function**: A function that takes either one or more functions as input, and returns a function as its output.
- **Inheritance**: An object-oriented programming capability that allows one class to inherit member variables and methods from another class.
- **Lambda expressions**: See Anonymous function.
- **Lazy evaluation**: A computer language evaluation strategy that delays the evaluation of an expression until its value is needed. The opposite of this strategy is called eager evaluation or greedy evaluation. Lazy evaluation is also known as call by need.
- **Library**: A set of objects and functions that have a well-defined interface that allows a third-party program to invoke their behavior.
- **Memoization**: The technique of storing the results of expensive function calls. When the function is called later with the same arguments, the stored result is returned rather than computing the result again.
- **Method chain**: A pattern in which many methods are invoked side by side by directly passing the output of one method to the input of the next. This avoids the need to assign the intermediary values to temporary variables.
- **Mixin**: An object that can allow other objects to use its methods. The methods are intended to be used solely by other objects, and the mixin object itself is never to be instantiated.
- **Modularity**: The degree to which a program can be broken down into independent modules of code. Functional programming increases the modularity of programs.
- **Monad**: A structure that provides the encapsulation required by functors.

- **Morphism**: A pure function that only works on a certain category and always returns the same output when given a specific set of inputs. Homomorphic operations are restricted to a single category, while polymorphic operations can operate on multiple categories.
- **Partial application**: The process of binding values to one or more arguments of a function. It returns a partially applied function, which in turn accepts the remaining, unbound arguments.
- **Polyfill**: A function used to augment prototypes with new functions. It allows us to call our new functions as methods of the previous function.
- **Pure function**: A function whose output value depends only on the arguments that are the input to the function. Thus, calling a function, f, twice with the same value of an argument, x, will produce the same result, $f(x)$, every time.
- **Recursive function**: A function that calls itself. Such functions depend on solutions to smaller instances of the same problem to compute the solution to the larger problem. Like iteration, recursion is another way to repeatedly call the same block of code. But, unlike iteration, recursion requires that the code block define the case in which the repeating code calls should terminate, known as the base case.
- **Reusability**: The degree to which a block of code, usually a function in JavaScript, can be reused in other parts of the same program or in other programs.
- **Self-invoking function**: An anonymous function that is invoked immediately after it has been defined. In JavaScript, this is achieved by placing a pair of parentheses after the function expression.
- **Strategy pattern**: A method used to define a family of interchangeable algorithms.
- **Tail recursion**: A stack-based implementation of recursion. For every recursive call, there is a new frame in the stack.
- **Toolkit**: A small software library that provides a set of functions for the programmer to use. Compared to a library, a toolkit is simpler and requires less coupling with the program that invokes it.
- **Trampolining**: A strategy for recursion that provides tail-call elimination in programming languages that do not provide this feature, such as JavaScript.
- **Y-combinator**: A fixed-point combinator in Lambda calculus that eliminates explicit recursion. When it is given as input to a function that returns a recursive function, the Y-combinator returns the fixed point of that function, which is the transformation from the recursive function to a non-recursive function.

Index

A

anonymous functions 21-23, 143
arrayOf functor 85
arrays 84

B

backbone.js 1
Bacon.js 45
Bilby.js 42-44
bind() function 55
bluebird 91

C

C++
  versus JavaScript 121
callback 143
call() function 55
categories
  about 79
  implementing 95-98
category theory
  about 78-80, 143
  objects 82, 83
  type safety functions, creating 80-82
classical mixins 129
Clojure 1, 99
closure
  about 19, 143
  using 19
CoffeeScript 99
Command Line Interface (CLI) 50

common functions, functional programming 135-140
compose
  programming with 65-68
coupling 143
currying 54, 60, 61, 143

D

declarative programming 143
development environment 48
discrete mathematics 78
Dojo 1

E

ease.js 15
e-commerce website application
  about 2
  imperative methods 2-4
endofunctors 94, 144
engines 16
environments, JavaScript applications
  browsers 48
  Command Line Interface (CLI) 50
  server-side JavaScript 49
European Computer Manufacturers Association (ECMAScript) 16

F

Fantasy Land 41, 42
filter() function
  parameters 30

forEach() function
  parameters 33
functional inheritance
  about 125, 126
  Strategy Pattern 126, 127
functional language
  about 144
  compiling, into JavaScript 51
functional libraries
  using 50
functional libraries, for JavaScript
  about 38
  Bacon.js 45
  Bilby.js 42, 44
  Boiler.js 47
  Fantasy Land 41, 42
  Folktale 47
  Functional 46
  from.js 47
  jQuery 47
  JSLINQ 47
  Lazy.js 44, 45
  Lo-Dash.js 46
  sloth.js 46
  Sugar 47
  stream.js 46
  Underscore.js 38-41
  wu.js 46
functional mixins 130-132
functional programming
  about 1, 4, 6, 68, 69, 144
  and object-oriented programming, mixing 125
  events, handling 70, 71
  used, in nonfunctional programming 14, 15
functional programming languages
  about 9
  advantages 11-14
  characteristics 10
  JavaScript 15, 16
  performing 10
functional programming, using object-oriented programming
  functional inheritance 125, 126
  mixins 128, 129

Functional Reactive Programming (FRP)
  about 71, 72, 144
  reactivity 72, 73
  subscriber, modifying 73-75
function composition
  about 62, 85, 86, 144
  compose() 62, 63
  compositions, versus chains 64, 65
  rewriting 86, 87
  sequence, using 63
function constructor 115, 116
function declarations
  about 114
  versus function expressions 115-117
function expressions
  about 115
  versus function constructor 115, 116
function factories 56, 57
function manipulation
  about 54
  apply() function 54
  bind() function 55
  call() function 55
  function factories 56, 57
  this keyword 54
functions
  anonymous functions 21-23
  closures, using 18, 19
  higher-order functions 19
  lazy evaluation 26
  methods, chaining 23, 24
  pure functions 20, 21
  recursive function 24, 25
  self-invoking function, using 18, 19
  working with 17
function statements. *See* **function declarations**
functors
  about 83, 144
  creating 84
  function compositions 85, 86

G

global scope, variables 110

H

Haskell 10
higher-order functions 19, 144
homomorphic operations 79

I

identity function morphism 85
inheritance
  about 121, 122, 144
  with Object.create() method 123, 124

J

JavaScript
  about 1, 15, 99
  function constructor 114
  function declarations 114
  function expressions 114
  multi-paradigm language 120
  object-oriented implementation 121
  recursion 100
  variable scope 109
  versus C++ 121
jQuery 1
jQuery object
  about 94
  implementing 94, 95
Julia 1

L

lazy evaluation
  about 26, 144
  benefits 27
Lazy.js 44, 45
lenses 92
lens() function
  writing 93
library 144
LINQ (Language Integrated Query) 47
Lisp 10, 77
local scope, variables 110, 111

M

map() function
  parameters 29
maybes
  about 88-90
  writing 88
memoization
  about 108, 109, 144
  reference link 108
method chain 144
mixins
  about 128, 129, 144
  classical mixins 129
  functional mixins 130-132
modularity 144
monads
  about 87, 144
  jQuery object 94
  lenses 92
  maybes 88
  promises 91
morphisms 79, 80, 82, 145
MVP (model-view-provider) 50

O

Object.create() method
  using 123
object-oriented implementation, JavaScript
  inheritance 121, 122
  inheritance, with Object.create() method 123, 124
  prototype chain 122
  prototypes, using 121
object-oriented programming
  and functional programming, mixing 125
object properties, variables 111
objects 80

P

partial application
  about 54, 57, 145
  left arguments, applying 58, 59
  right arguments, applying 59

polyadic 62
polyfill 145
polymorphic operations 79
production environment 48
promises
  using 91
prototype chain 122
prototypes
  using, for inheritance 121
pure functions 20, 21, 145
pyjamas 99
Pyjs 51
Python 1

Q

QuickCheck 43

R

recursion
  about 100
  Y-Combinator 106, 107
recursive function
  about 24, 25, 145
  Divide and Conquer 25, 26
reduce() function
  parameters 31
reusability 145
Roy 51
Ruby 1

S

ScalaCheck 43
Scheme 10, 77
scope resolutions
  about 109
  global scope 110
  local scope 110, 111
  object properties 111
self-invoking function
  about 145
  using 18
server-side JavaScript
  functional use case 49, 50
Strategy Pattern 126, 127

T

tail-call elimination
  about 101, 102
  trampolining 103-105
tail recursion
  about 100, 101, 145
  tail-call elimination 101, 102
ternary 62
this keyword 54
thunks 103-105
toolkit 145
toolkit, functional programmer
  about 27, 28
  Array.prototype.concat 33
  Array.prototype.every 35
  Array.prototype.filter() 30
  Array.prototype.forEach 32
  Array.prototype.map() 29, 30
  Array.prototype.reduce() 31, 32
  Array.prototype.reverse 34
  Array.prototype.some 35
  Array.prototype.sort 34
  callbacks, using 28
trampolining 16, 103-105, 145
TypeScript 51

U

UHC 51
unary functions 62
underscore.js 1, 38-41

V

variable scope
  about 109
  features 113, 114
  issues 112, 113
  scope resolutions 109
variadic 62

Y

Y-Combinator
  about 106, 107, 145
  memoization 108, 109

Thank you for buying
Functional Programming in JavaScript

About Packt Publishing
Packt, pronounced 'packed', published its first book, *Mastering phpMyAdmin for Effective MySQL Management*, in April 2004, and subsequently continued to specialize in publishing highly focused books on specific technologies and solutions.

Our books and publications share the experiences of your fellow IT professionals in adapting and customizing today's systems, applications, and frameworks. Our solution-based books give you the knowledge and power to customize the software and technologies you're using to get the job done. Packt books are more specific and less general than the IT books you have seen in the past. Our unique business model allows us to bring you more focused information, giving you more of what you need to know, and less of what you don't.

Packt is a modern yet unique publishing company that focuses on producing quality, cutting-edge books for communities of developers, administrators, and newbies alike. For more information, please visit our website at www.packtpub.com.

About Packt Open Source
In 2010, Packt launched two new brands, Packt Open Source and Packt Enterprise, in order to continue its focus on specialization. This book is part of the Packt Open Source brand, home to books published on software built around open source licenses, and offering information to anybody from advanced developers to budding web designers. The Open Source brand also runs Packt's Open Source Royalty Scheme, by which Packt gives a royalty to each open source project about whose software a book is sold.

Writing for Packt
We welcome all inquiries from people who are interested in authoring. Book proposals should be sent to author@packtpub.com. If your book idea is still at an early stage and you would like to discuss it first before writing a formal book proposal, then please contact us; one of our commissioning editors will get in touch with you.

We're not just looking for published authors; if you have strong technical skills but no writing experience, our experienced editors can help you develop a writing career, or simply get some additional reward for your expertise.

Mastering JavaScript Design Patterns

ISBN: 978-1-78398-798-6   Paperback: 290 pages

Discover how to use JavaScript design patterns to create powerful applications with reliable and maintainable code

1. Learn how to use tried and true software design methodologies to enhance your JavaScript code.
2. Discover robust JavaScript implementations of classic as well as advanced design patterns.
3. Packed with easy-to-follow examples that can be used to create reusable code and extensible designs.

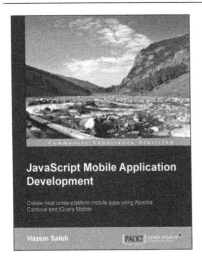

JavaScript Mobile Application Development

ISBN: 978-1-78355-417-1   Paperback: 332 pages

Create neat cross-platform mobile apps using Apache Cordova and jQuery Mobile

1. Configure your Android, iOS, and Window Phone 8 development environments.
2. Extend the power of Apache Cordova by creating your own Apache Cordova cross-platform mobile plugins.
3. Enhance the quality and the robustness of your Apache Cordova mobile application by unit testing its logic using Jasmine.

Please check **www.PacktPub.com** for information on our titles

Learning JavaScript Data Structures and Algorithms

ISBN: 978-1-78355-487-4 Paperback: 218 pages

Understand and implement classic data structures and algorithms using JavaScript

1. Learn how to use the most used data structures such as array, stack, list, tree, and graphs with real-world examples.

2. Get a grasp on which one is best between searching and sorting algorithms and learn how to implement them.

3. Follow through solutions for notable programming problems with step-by-step explanations.

JavaScript Promises Essentials

ISBN: 978-1-78398-564-7 Paperback: 90 pages

Build fully functional web applications using Promises, the new standard in JavaScript

1. Integrate JavaScript Promises into your application by mastering the key concepts of the Promises API.

2. Replace complex nested callbacks in JavaScript with the more intuitive chained Promises.

3. Acquire the knowledge needed to start working with JavaScript Promises immediately.

Please check **www.PacktPub.com** for information on our titles

Lightning Source UK Ltd.
Milton Keynes UK
UKOW05f1810040116

265759UK00001B/33/P